$\mathcal{R}$ising

Learning from Women's Leadership in Catholic Ministries

CAROLYN Y. WOO, PhD

Blessings,
Carolyn Woo

ORBIS BOOKS
Maryknoll, New York 10545

Founded in 1970, Orbis Books endeavors to publish works that enlighten the mind, nourish the spirit, and challenge the conscience. The publishing arm of the Maryknoll Fathers and Brothers, Orbis seeks to explore the global dimensions of the Christian faith and mission, to invite dialogue with diverse cultures and religious traditions, and to serve the cause of reconciliation and peace. The books published reflect the views of their authors and do not represent the official position of the Maryknoll Society. To learn more about Maryknoll and Orbis Books, please visit our website at www.orbisbooks.com.

Manufactured in the United States of America.
Manuscript editing and typesetting by Joan Weber Laflamme.

Library of Congress Cataloging-in-Publication Data

Names: Woo, Carolyn Y., author.
Title: Rising : learning from women's leadership in Catholic ministries / Carolyn Y. Woo.
Description: Maryknoll, NY : Orbis Books, [2022] | Includes bibliographical references. | Summary: "Lessons from the experience of Catholic women in leadership in a wide range of Catholic ministries"— Provided by publisher.
Identifiers: LCCN 2021039958 (print) | LCCN 2021039959 (ebook) | ISBN 9781626984738 (print) | ISBN 9781608339358 (epub)
Subjects: LCSH: Women in church work—Catholic Church. | Christian leadership—Catholic Church.
Classification: LCC BX2347.8.W6 W68 2022 (print) | LCC BX2347.8.W6 (ebook) | DDC 282.082—dc23
LC record available at https://lccn.loc.gov/2021039958
LC ebook record available at https://lccn.loc.gov/2021039959

To the Maryknoll Sisters

Thank you for being my first teachers and continuing role models in faith. By your teaching, I developed my voice. Watching you, I learned how that voice is to be used. God first became real to me because God is real to you. In your eyes and ministries, joy sparkles. Know that we, the Maryknoll Girls, live in your spirit of compassion, friendship, and trust in God. What is in you is now in us.

*G*od has yet a great work for us to do, but the realization of this vision depends on you and me as individuals and on our cooperation. Do we love enough, do we work enough, do we pray enough, do we suffer enough? . . . Our future depends on our answer.

—MOTHER MARY JOSEPH,
FOUNDER OF THE MARYKNOLL SISTERS

Contents

Contents

Part IV
Reflections on Leadership

Introduction

A Long Time Coming

Years before I committed thoughts to paper on the topic of women's leadership in the Catholic Church, I had been writing this book in my head. The issue follows me like a shadow. At almost every talk, even when women leading was not the featured topic, the interest was there. In over five hundred speeches in a span of twenty years, women leading in the church was the featured headline on no more than ten occasions. Yet there was always an undercurrent of curiosity of how a woman became the dean of the Business School at the University of Notre Dame and then chief executive officer of Catholic Relief Services, the official international humanitarian agency of the US Catholic Church.

That curiosity is on two fronts. First is the personal story of how a Chinese immigrant from Hong Kong navigated the journeys to these positions. The second point of interest pivots on the experience of a woman in leadership within the Catholic hierarchies governed by ordained clergy. How does this happen? What is it like? Is this path accessible to others? The first is a story I have told in an earlier book, *Working for a Better World*. The second is the motivation for this current book.

Lodged in my mind is the evening of a public conversation titled "Women Taking the Lead: Acting on Pope Francis'

Message."[1] A conversation ensued after the program, one that I have been trying to finish ever since that evening. Surrounding me at the foot of the stage was a group of young women who were students from a local Catholic high school. Minutes into the conversation one asked, "Dr. Woo, do you think women's leadership in the church is really possible beyond exceptions because it seems that women are not welcomed by the church and there are no doors that we can even knock on?"

I winced as I took in the students' faces. Their countenances reflected light and infinite potential. The student's question was nothing but earnestness, though its tone vibrated with dejection. Without hesitation, I blurted: "No, no, no: there are many opportunities for women. You must not be discouraged. You must. . . ." The conversation ended abruptly as my attention was hijacked by someone seeking a selfie and the students needed to board their bus.

Over the years I have continued to ponder what answer these young women and many like them, the future of our church, deserve. A jangle of contrasting thoughts fights for articulation.

Without doubt, the case of women leading in Catholic Church ministries is regarded as a rarity. Foreclosure of priestly ordination to women has generated an unshakable and widely held conclusion that the Catholic Church does not value women, appreciate what they have to contribute, or trust and empower them to help shape church doctrines, policies, and ministries.

Women's leadership in the Catholic Church is a fraught topic that has spawned panels, dialogs, and conferences. The conversation at Georgetown that evening featured three women leaders: Sr. Carol Keehan (chief executive officer of Catholic Health Association), Sr. Donna Markham (executive director of Catholic

---

[1] "Women Taking the Lead: Acting on Pope Francis' Message," sponsored by the Initiative on Catholic Social Thought and Public Life, Berkeley Center for Religion, Peace & World Affairs, Georgetown University, October 22, 2015.

Charities USA), and myself (chief executive officer and president of Catholic Relief Services).

The assembly of the three leaders on the dais was described as historical for the unprecedented coincidence that three of the largest ministries of the US Catholic Church were simultaneously helmed by women. Surely, this would not be considered historical if three men were on the stage. This assembly of three women leaders was of sufficient interest to pack the assembly hall and drew many Catholic women's groups, including the girls' Catholic high school for an evening outing on a school night.

While this student's question and many other similar expressions troubled me, I am grateful for them. They are disconcerting and vexing, but at least they are being raised. What I fear more than these discordant notes is silence: the silence that follows when women finally give up asking, pursuing, challenging, advocating, or voicing their expectations. Of great concern to me is the resignation that settles in when young women no longer knock because the interest no longer registers and they walk past the doors, open or padlocked.

A Pew report found that the percentage of Catholics in the United States has dropped from 24 percent in 2007 to 21 percent in 2014. Of the US adult population, 13 percent are former Catholics.[2] A 2018 survey of 1508 women self-identified as Catholic by *America* finds that 18 percent of the respondents have thought of leaving or actually left for a period of time. Of these individuals, about half cite the treatment of women as "somewhat" or "very much" a concern.[3]

When asked whether or not they have experienced sexism in the church, 10 percent said yes. Of note is that those who

---

[2] David Masci and Gregory A. Smith, "7 Facts about American Catholics," Pew Research Center, October 10, 2018.

[3] Mark M. Gray and Mary L. Gautier, "Catholic Women in the United States: Practices, Experiences, and Attitudes," Center for Applied Research in the Apostolate, commissioned by America/Media (2018), 13.

attended a Catholic college or university (25 percent), those who considered becoming a religious sister or nun (23 percent), those who attended a Catholic high school (16 percent), and those who have served in a parish ministry role (15 percent) were more likely to respond yes to the question.[4]

Tough medicine. As feedback is often a gift, it would be advisable to approach these more critical groups with humility, attention, and optimism. These individuals speak from deep attachment to the church. They are invested in learning about the church and seeking an active role. They have not thrown up their hands, shrugged their shoulders, or turned their backs. These women care and love enough to endure their disappointments, to continue to call for and believe in what is possible. These women assume the emotional burden of expecting more. Invite them: that should be our response.

In a study commissioned by FADICA (Foundations and Donors Interested in Catholic Activities),[5] the engagement of women, both lay and religious sisters, is proposed as one of four critical social innovations to have the most impact on the vitality of parishes going forward. Recommendations identified three other areas of priorities: youth engagement, engagement of Hispanics, and a more welcoming church.

The report speaks with utmost urgency on the topic of women. Three factors contribute to this conclusion: (1) nearly 80 percent of the staff in parish ministries are women, (2) these women are getting older with the average age of parish staff at fifty-five years, and (3) the flow of applicants would be more aptly described as a talent trickle than a talent pool.

It has been noted that the exclusion of women is akin to walking on one leg, seeing with one eye, breathing with one lung, operating with one side of the brain. Chittister gives us

---

[4] Gray and Gautier, 15–16.

[5] Marti R. Jewel and Mark Mogilka, "Open Wide the Doors to Christ: A Study of Catholic Social Innovation for Parish Vitality," FADICA (2020), 17–18.

pause as she asks, "Can the Church possibly be whole without women?"[6]

Pope Francis answers, "A Church without women can't be understood."[7]

While the dismissal of women is the dominant narrative, I do not hold the view that women's leadership in the Catholic Church is as rare, unusual, and out of reach as the perceptions held by many people inside and outside of the church. In over twenty years of leading two Catholic institutions and serving on boards of about fifteen more, I have interacted with many women who play such roles. One can draw up a list of such individuals to populate a monthly program of women leaders over multiple years. These include leaders, founders, and board members in all sectors of Catholic ministries such as K-12 education, higher education, social services, health ministries, pastoral ministries, diocesan administration, clergy formation, communications, and advocacy.

While leadership appointments for women can be significantly expanded, and misogyny still dishonors women and brushes aside their gifts, it is important to acknowledge the inroads that have been made and opportunities that are accessible to women. Perceptions and general criticisms have not kept pace with emerging reality, which points to a notable number of women leading with impact and influence.

Perceptions harden into judgments that can lead to unfortunate choices. A college-age daughter of a good friend and devout Catholic challenges her mother, "Why would I give my life to a church that does not welcome me, value my gift, give me a chance?" Logical conclusion, but from a wrong premise. Though not universal and far from sufficient in attitude and action, there

---

[6] Joan Chittister, OSB, *Women Strength: Modern Church, Modern Women* (Kansas City, MO: Sheed and Ward, 1990), 12.

[7] Pope Francis, "Apostolic Journey to Rio de Janeiro on the Occasion of the XXVIII World Youth Day," press conference during the return flight, July 28, 2013.

is evidence that women are not locked out wholesale from positions of authority in Catholic ministries.

We must not lose this young woman from the church because of misinformation. We need her gifts, her voice, and her passion to be part of a community that witnesses to the presence of God here and now. We need her to act from the love she receives from the body of Christ and direct this to those who hunger for it. We want her to know that she is made by God to do things that only she can do. We should not make it easy for her to turn away, without a monumental struggle, from her baptismal call and responsibility as prophet, priest, and sovereign. To the women who are discouraged: I hope this book motivates you to reassess and commit.

In setting the record straight, I hope to convey a note of thanks, long overdue, to the many women leaders whose service has sustained the vitality and viability of many Catholic ministries. No, they did not do it on their own, but in the company of the Holy Spirit. We thank them for welcoming the Holy Spirit when they stood alone.

Focus of the Book

The focus of this book on formal leaders by no means dismisses all the women who have served the church as parishioners, volunteers for different ministries, and the staff who make the programs run. It is important to clarify that leadership can occur at every level of organizations and in every function. Titles are not necessary for the exercise of leadership. Indeed, the Catholic Church has run on the labor, passion, and commitments of such individuals, many nameless, to do its work of evangelization, formation, service, and community building.

I intend our attention on women leaders to be an acknowledgment of all women who serve the church. Leadership appointments suggest that women are not valued simply for their labor and support, but also for their voice and talents that sometimes result in positions of influence and impact. Increasingly, what women have to offer is coming into view, their desire to be engaged as full members of the body of Christ is being heeded, and their rightful place at the family table is being set.

This book pivots on formal leaders because their appointments reflect explicit power-sharing arrangements between the institutional church and women. This step is categorically different from welcoming hardworking volunteers and junior staff who remain "guests" or "outsiders," not people who shape the future of the organization.

Formal leaders enjoy the legitimacy to weigh in and participate as an integral part of the decision-making process on critical issues. Their inclusion is an acknowledgment that women, as well as men, have the capacity and talent to lead. Being offered the mantle of leadership derives from respect and trust. It represents an investment, a conferral of power, beyond mere intent, words, or pats on the back.

I should clarify that power should never be the motivator for ministry. But formal power is one kind of currency to bring about change, call for improvement, gain the floor, and mobilize resources. To the extent that this currency is given to men, it should also be made available to women for similar purposes.

The many leadership positions that women now occupy would not be possible without active sponsorship by the priests and bishops who opened up the space. To be fair, we have not acknowledged the hospitality, invitations, and investments that raised women to chancellors, chief operating and financial officers, canon lawyers, superintendents, and so on. We do not know what battles were waged for the appointment of women to assignments traditionally held by men or positions that supervise clergy.

We underestimate what goes on behind the scenes to change cultures so that women can flourish in these contexts. There is no question that more is needed. But it should not obscure the efforts made by some clergy through their vision, goodwill, and action. I hope this book on women's leadership in the church will show what has worked, what more is needed, what opportunities can be placed within reach of women, and how co-responsibility can be cultivated.

This book is my attempt to circle back to the unfinished conversation with the student at the Georgetown seminar. I want her to know why she should not dismiss a place for her service in the church, why it is not a fool's errand to pursue her work life within the church, and how her contributions and commitments can help bring about the peaceable kingdom that Jesus started. And yes, she can find respect, appreciation, partnership, and fulfillment in this choice.

Organization of the Book

The next five chapters compose Part One of the book: "Women's Leadership in Catholic Ministries." Chapter 1 lists four misperceptions that get in the way of women seriously considering professional work in the church: (1) few leadership opportunities are available to women in Catholic ministries; (2) church leaders do not advocate for women's leadership; (3) lay ministry is subordinated to ordained ministry; and (4) women are not well suited for leadership roles in Catholic ministries.

Chapter 2 highlights the common attributes of sixteen women leaders I have recruited to enlarge my own views. The synthesis produced five attributes: (1) they are compelled to serve those in need; (2) they are committed to their staffs; (3) they take ownership of problems; (4) they seek to bridge and heal differences; and (5) their work is rooted in faith.

Chapter 3 delves into the challenges that women and lay people face in church ministries. The first two challenges relate to the struggles women face under these sections: (1) co-responsibility: early in the journey, and (2) woman: the outsider.

The last two sections describe challenges faced by church ministries in general: (3) negotiating differences with church hierarchy; and (4) navigating cultural hotspots.

Chapter 4 provides a reflection on the concept of feminine genius proposed by a number of recent popes. Though well intentioned, this categorization can be problematic and can work against women. The chapter presents the reasons for caution. I also offer a few words on the concepts of power and control as these seem to create great discomfort and dissonance for women.

The last chapter (Chapter 5) in this section issues a call for action noting the changes needed and resources available for welcoming women into ministries and supporting their success. The chapter is divided into (1) what church ministries can do; (2) resources for women's development; and (3) planting the seeds early in girls and female young adults for eventual participation in church ministries.

Part Two, "Requisite Capacities for Leadership," discusses what I see as necessary qualities to leadership for all people, regardless of gender and type of organization. These draw on my four decades of teaching, research, and practice of strategic leadership. They emanate from lessons of both successes and deficiencies. These include (1) capacity for the other; (2) capacity for self-awareness and growth; and (3) capacity for alignment. These are located in Chapters 6 to 8, respectively. Chapter 9 presents a capacity that is unique to faith-based ministries: the capacity for Christian witness. Faith-based ministries do not just perform good works—these emanate from the love of Christ and point to his presence amid us. As both Pope Benedict and Pope Francis have cautioned, the essence of our ministries is not just charitable impulse.

In Part Three, "Journeys of Leadership in Catholic Ministries," I incorporate the voices of sixteen other women leaders in various Catholic ministries. Each leader contributes a personal essay that describes the unique ways she heard and followed the vocational summons into ministry. These reflections compose a broad portfolio of paths, backgrounds, choices, and styles by which leadership unfolds and evolves. Each woman, however, reached beyond the "known" to find herself in the company of the Holy Spirit. Chapters 10 to 26 depict love stories written through the intersection of faith and work.

In recruiting women leaders for this book, I wanted to make sure we draw from diverse ministries, roles, races, and ages. Some ministries are part of diocesan structures; one is governed by the United States Conference of Catholic Bishops (USCCB); some are apostolates of religious orders; and a number are start-ups. Including myself, the group comprises three religious sisters and fourteen lay people. The roles they hold span principal, executive director, president, executive vice president, editor, and board member. Of these women leaders, three are Asian Americans and one is Hispanic. Unfortunately, two leaders, one Hispanic and one African American, had to step out of the project due to personal reasons.

I also invited these leaders to be my thought partners on the chapter themes presented in Part One. I presented a set of questions to which they offered written responses. These will not be published except for some quotations excerpted from their essays. There are two exceptions. The responses by Jennifer Fiduccia and Sr. Donna Markham are especially moving, and I have included them in full in Part Four.

The message to readers is that there is not just one path, one mold, one set of qualifications and skills, or one common approach. These narratives showcase differences and uniqueness, highlighting how we can be true to ourselves, utilize our different gifts, and build from our own life experiences to navigate how we respond to God's call in our own way.

PART I

WOMEN'S LEADERSHIP
IN CATHOLIC MINISTRIES

1

Misperceptions about Women's Leadership in Catholic Ministries

The Catholic Church's relationship with women is fraught and frequently presented in tones which are difficult, painful, and even adversarial. Depictions often unfold within the context of women being precluded from ordination. Equally dispiriting are the descriptions of women diminished in their interactions with clergy. One does not have to reach far to point out the dominance of men in key decision-making roles in different Catholic institutions. Many women colleagues in church ministries can recount instances when they and their ideas were dismissed because of their gender and lay status. These challenges are real and will be addressed in a later chapter of this book.

At the same time we must guard against an unquestioned and wholesale generalization that the Catholic Church does not value the gifts of women, offers no opportunities for leadership, precludes women from making or influencing significant decisions, or closes them off from shaping the ways that we, the body of Christ, step up to help build the kingdom of God here and now. The mistreatment is true in some cases, but not in all cases.

There are needs crying out for the service and leadership of women outside the scope of ordained ministries. To dismiss

these is to ignore the hurts and deprivations where people labor
without the essentials for human dignity or the compassion and
companionship that make God real. To focus only on ordained
ministries unnecessarily restricts the opportunities to render
God's love palpable and put hope within reach. It is clericalism
we inflict on ourselves.

While we should not ignore past grievances, we should also
open our hearts to acknowledge corrective steps when these
have been put in place as steppingstones to a new path. Holding onto a narrative of only "wrongs" does not do justice to the
hospitality and right of way that have been extended. Neither
does it serve women, particularly those seriously searching, to
heed their call to service in the church. Our grievance does not
point out the doors and invitations to ministries that are calling
for women's gifts and commitment. Most concerning is when
my friend's college-age daughter acts from the premise that the
church does not value her or women in general. We must counter the misperceptions and not simply accede to our individual
and collective wounds.

The discussion below counters four common misperceptions.

Misperception 1: Few Leadership Opportunities Are Available to Women in Catholic Ministries

The general accusation that the church just does not invite
women into leadership positions with significant impact is over-
stated. Many examples illustrate otherwise. In the church, women
serve as chancellors, chief operating officers, chief finance officers,
or planning directors of dioceses. For example, a young woman
in her thirties undertook the functions to assess parish financial
health, identify ways for improvement, make recommendations
for capital projects, and implement parish consolidation and
closures. Most directors of parish pastoral ministries and religious
education are women. Catholic K-12 education would not be

able to function without women principals and superintendents. Many Catholic universities are presided over by women. The social service and health associations represented by Sr. Donna Markham and Sr. Carol Keehan in this volume rely heavily on women to run their respective agencies and Catholic hospitals. Women have also been charged to shape and disseminate the messaging of the Catholic Church as diocesan directors of communication and editors of publications. Boards for advisory, review, and governance purposes are frequently populated and chaired by women.

The Catholic ministries led or governed by the women in this book include a school, university, health system, national associations, lobbying organization, parish faith formation ministry, leadership development of church personnel, US and international social service, women's care center, and public media.

From 2011 to 2021 the percent of women CEOs in Catholic health systems rose from 27 percent to 34 percent.[1] Of the Catholic universities which are members of the American Catholic Colleges and Universities, 34 percent are led by women.[2] As of 2021, the percentages of women serving as staff, principals, and superintendents at Catholic schools are 77, 67, and 49 percent, respectively.[3] Of the local Catholic Charities agencies, 47 percent are led by women.[4] The Catholic Media Association consists of 854 members. Of those, 462 are women with about 200 holding titles of president, editor, vice president, director, coordinator, and manager of communication.[5]

A survey commissioned almost twenty years ago by the Leadership Conference of Women Religious (LCWR) shows

---

[1] Kim Hewitt, Catholic Health Association, July 14, 2021.

[2] Rebecca Sawyer, American Catholic Colleges and Universities, July 14, 2021.

[3] Annie Smith, National Catholic Education Association, July 9, 2021.

[4] Sr. Donna Markham, Catholic Charities USA, July 15, 2021.

[5] From Tim Walter, Catholic Media Association, July 20, 2021.

that "Catholic women—married, single, and religious sisters—are already participating in the administration of the Catholic Church by making high-level executive decisions affecting church personnel, property, and policy." The survey examines the exercise of jurisdiction (the power of governance) by women in six roles within the US church. These are chancellor, tribunal judge, diocesan finance director, director of Catholic Charities, vicar/delegate for religious, and pastoral director of a parish.[6]

Findings are drawn from in-depth interviews with twenty-five women who hold these positions in twenty-four dioceses. These interviews are supplemented by survey responses from women operating in these roles across all dioceses. Three out of four survey recipients provided responses. Results indicate that women are systematically making critical decisions affecting church operations. Of these, personnel and church property are the most common. The study thus manages to "demystify the concept of jurisdiction, demonstrate the dimensions already in practice, and identify possibilities for enhancing the contributions of non-ordained persons in church governance."[7]

The appointment of women to senior positions has also been taking place at the Vatican. Notable is the appointment of six women in August 2020 to provide oversight of Vatican finances and budgets as members of the Council for the Economy.[8] The council is led by a cardinal and fourteen members: seven ordained clergy and seven lay people. That nearly all lay slots are assigned to women is an important step toward raising the profile and authority of women at the Holy See.

---

[6] Anne Munley, IHM, et al., "Women and Jurisdiction: An Unfolding Reality," The LCWR Study of Selected Church Leadership Roles, Leadership Conference of Women Religious, 2001.

[7] "Study Reveals Women's Decision-Making Roles in the Church," *National Catholic Reporter Online* 38, no. 19 (March 15, 2002).

[8] "Pope Chooses Six Women as Lay Experts for Council for the Economy," *Vatican News*, August 6, 2020.

On International Women's Day in March 2020, *Vatican News* reported that from 2010 to 2019 the Holy See (not including Vatican City) increased the number of women employed from 385 to 649, almost a 70 percent increase. The number of women appointed to senior positions as undersecretaries in the dicasteries rose to four in 2019 compared with two at the beginning of the decade. In total, the number of women in high-ranking managerial administrative positions, including the director of the Vatican Museum, grew three-fold from three to nine at the Vatican over this period.[9]

In 2021, Pope Francis made four high-profile appointments of women. In February, Sr. Nathalie Becquart was designated as one of two undersecretaries of the Synod of Bishops. She will be the first woman to be able to vote in the synod. A month later, Sr. Nutria Calduch-Benages was appointed secretary of the Vatican Biblical Commission, a consultative body that focuses on the proper interpretation of Sacred Scriptures. Emilee Cuda was named the head of the office of the Pontifical Commission for Latin America. Salesian sister Alessandra Smerilli will serve as interim Secretary of the Dicastery for Promoting Integral Human Development.

There is no question that much more can be done. On the other hand, a sweeping negation of leadership opportunities to women is unsupported. To the young women at Georgetown who asked if my rise to leadership is an exception, my answer would be no. It is not an exception, but it is not yet the norm.

Misperception 2: Church Leaders Do Not Advocate for Women's Leadership in Catholic Ministries

There is a general sense that women's talents are often dismissed, that they are seldom noted or actively solicited by church leaders.

---

[9] "Number of Women Employees in the Vatican on the Rise," *Vatican News*, March 6, 2020.

Spoken or not, the underlying presumption of many women is that the church hierarchy relegates women to their "proper" places as volunteers or support staff: good people who are diligent, reliable, and agreeable.

Over the last fifty years, despite, or perhaps because of, the foreclosure of priestly ordination to women, the Vatican has explicitly proclaimed the importance and gifts of women. In his December 8, 1965, address to women at the closing of Vatican II, Pope Paul VI noted: "Women, you know how to make the truth sweet, tender, and accessible. . . . Make it your task to bring the spirit of this Council into institutions, schools, homes, and daily life. Women of the entire universe, whether Christian or non-believing, you to whom life is entrusted at this grave moment in history, it is for you to save the world."

In *Mulieris Dignitatem,* St. Pope John Paul II states that the foundation for the genius of women emanates from Mary, a woman, who is at the center of the salvific event, thus manifesting the "extraordinary dignity of the woman" (no. 4). The manifestation of this feminine genius imparts sensitivity to others in all circumstances which in turn shapes relationships and society.

In his letter to women on June 29, 1995, Pope John Paul II again speaks of this "genius":

> In this vast domain of service, the Church's two-thousand-year history, for all its historical conditioning, has truly experienced the "genius of women"; from the heart of the Church there have emerged women of the highest calibre who have left an impressive and beneficial mark in history. . . . And how can we overlook the many women, inspired by faith, who were responsible for initiatives of extraordinary social importance, especially in serving the poorest of the poor? The life of the Church in the Third Millennium will certainly not be lacking in new and surprising manifestations of the "feminine genius."

Statements of gratitude and recognition are effusive. In *Mulieris Dignitatem* Pope John Paul II again offers his thanks:

> The witness and the achievements of Christian women have had a significant impact on the life of the Church as well as society. . . . In our own way the Church is constantly enriched by the witness of the many women who fulfil their vocation to holiness. . . . The Church gives thanks for all the manifestations of the feminine "genius" which have appeared in the course of history, in the midst of all peoples and nations; she gives thanks for all the charisms which the Holy Spirit distributes to women in the history of the People of God, for all the victories she owes to their faith, hope and charity: she gives thanks for all the fruits of feminine holiness. . . . The hour is coming, in fact has come, when the vocation of women is being acknowledged in its fullness, the hour in which women acquire in the world an influence, an effect and a power never hitherto achieved. (nos. 27, 31, 1)

Following his predecessors, Pope Francis continues the theme of "the feminine genius," describing women in terms of more developed intuition, attentiveness to others, compassion, and ability to see things with different eyes . . . to ask questions that men can't understand. In *Let Us Dream*,[10] Pope Francis describes the leadership of women as blessings in the midst of the global pandemic. He credits them with decisiveness and effective resolutions. He expresses deep gratitude for the women leaders of the world who acted with greater speed and clarity during the global pandemic.

---

[10] Pope Francis, conversation with Austin Ivereigh, *Let Us Dream: The Path to a Better Future* (New York: Simon and Schuster, 2020), 62–68.

Acknowledging that in practice many women have not enjoyed corresponding opportunities and engagement or have not been sought out in a manner aligned with the above statements, Pope John Paul II, in *Mulieris Dignitatem,* quotes Pope Paul VI, who stated, "It is evident that women are meant to form part of the living and working structure of Christianity in so prominent a manner that perhaps not all their potentialities have yet been made clear" (no. 1).[11]

In his June 25 letter to women prior to International Women's Day in 1995, Pope John Paul II admits to a sobering reality:

> I know of course that simply saying thank you is not enough. Unfortunately, we are heirs to a history which has *conditioned* us to a remarkable extent. In every time and place, this conditioning has been an obstacle to the progress of women. Women's dignity has often been unacknowledged and their prerogatives misrepresented; they have often been relegated to the margins of society and even reduced to servitude. This has prevented women from truly being themselves and it has resulted in a spiritual impoverishment of humanity. . . . And if objective blame, especially in particular historical contexts, has belonged to not just a few members of the Church, for this I am truly sorry. May this regret be transformed, on the part of the whole Church, into a renewed commitment of fidelity of the Gospel vision. . . . Let this genius be more fully expressed in the life of society as a whole, as well as in the life of the Church." (nos. 3, 1)

Echoing the same lament, Pope Francis emphasizes that

---

[11] Paul VI, "Address to the Participants in the National Congress of the Italian Woman Center (CIF) (December 6, 1976).

the role of women in the Church must not be limited to being mothers, workers, a limited role. . . . No! It is something else! . . . Paul VI wrote beautifully of women, but I believe that we have much more to do in making explicit this role and charism of women. We can't imagine a Church without women, but women active in the Church, with the distinctive role that they play.[12]

In his encyclical *Evangelii Gaudium* Pope Francis addresses this gap by calling for the incisive presence of women:

I readily acknowledge that many women share pastoral responsibilities with priests, helping to guide people, families and groups and offering new contributions to theological reflection. But we need to create still broader opportunities for a more incisive female presence in the Church. Because "the feminine genius is needed in all expressions in the life of society, the presence of women must also be guaranteed in the work place" and in the various other settings where important decisions are made, both in the Church and in social structures. (no. 103)

Again, at a general audience on April 15, 2015, Pope Francis reiterates, "It is necessary that women not only be listened to more, but that her voice carry real weight, a recognized authority in society and in the Church."

In strong words on another occasion, he notes: "[The] expanded role for women in Church leadership doesn't depend on the Vatican and is not limited to specific roles. Perhaps because of clericalism, which is a corruption of the priesthood, many people

---

[12] Pope Francis, "Apostolic Journey to Rio de Janeiro on the Occasion of the XXVIII World Youth Day," press conference during the return flight, July 28, 2013.

wrongly believe that Church leadership is exclusively male. . . .
To say that they aren't truly leaders because they aren't priests is
clericalism and disrespectful."[13]

To end this section, let us be reminded of the premise for
women's leadership stated by Pope John Paul II. In his June 25,
1995, letter to women he made it clear that the inclusion of
women is the imitation of Christ and, ultimately, an exercise of
justice and necessity:

> When it comes to setting women free from every kind of
> exploitation and domination, the Gospel contains an ever
> relevant message which goes back to the attitude of Jesus
> Christ himself. Transcending the established norms of his
> own culture, Jesus treated women with openness, respect,
> acceptance, and tenderness. . . . This is a matter of justice
> but also of necessity. . . . A greater presence of women in
> society will prove most valuable, for it will help to manifest
> the contradictions present when society is organized solely
> according to the criteria of efficiency and productivity, and
> it will force systems to be redesigned in a way which favors
> the processes of humanization which mark the "civilization
> of love. (nos. 3–4)

Misperception 3: Lay Ministry Is Subordinate to Ordained Ministry

Many lay people, men and women alike, presume incorrectly
that their ministries are subordinate to those of ordained ministers. Few recognize that lay people share a responsibility with
the clergy in the proclamation of the good news, witness to the
gospel, and service to neighbors.

---

[13] Pope Francis, *Let Us Dream,* 62–68.

Inclusion of women, respect for their points of view, and willingness to confer responsibility and authority do not require putting them on pedestals, highlighting their gifts in contrast to men's, or crowning them with the extraordinary attribution of "feminine genius." Acceptance and inclusion of women, as of all lay people, are grounded in their baptism.

The passages below teach clearly that in our baptism by water and the Holy Spirit we become a part of the one priesthood of Christ. Together with the ministerial priesthood, all the faithful are missionary disciples and share in the priestly, prophetic, and kingly roles of Jesus Christ. We are to live holy lives and actively commit to proclaiming God, participating in the divine plan of salvation for all.

From the Second Vatican Council, *Lumen Gentium* offers the following teaching on the laity and what our baptisms confer:

> The baptized, by regeneration and the anointing of the Holy Spirit, are consecrated as a spiritual house and a holy priesthood, in order that through all those works . . . they may offer spiritual sacrifices and proclaim the power of Him who has called them out of darkness into His marvelous light. Therefore all the disciples of Christ, persevering in prayer and praising God, should present themselves as a living sacrifice, holy and pleasing to God. (no. 10)
>
> These faithful [laity] are by baptism made one body with Christ and are constituted among the People of God; they are in their own way made sharers in the priestly, prophetical, and kingly functions of Christ; and they carry out for their own part the mission of the whole Christian people in the Church and in the world. . . . In this way they may make Christ known to others, especially by the testimony of a life resplendent in faith, hope and charity. (no. 31)

Upon all the laity, therefore, rests the noble duty of working to extend the divine plan of salvation to all men of each epoch and in every land. Consequently, may every opportunity be given them so that, according to their abilities and the needs of the times, they may zealously participate in the saving work of the Church. (no. 33)

The supreme and eternal Priest, Christ Jesus, since he wills to continue his witness and service also through the laity, vivifies them in this Spirit and increasingly urges them on to every good and perfect work. (no. 34)

Jennifer Fiduccia, the director of a pastoral ministry, illustrates in her chapter herein how she, empowered by her baptism, can carry out the priestly, prophetic, and kingly functions in meaningful ways:

Priest/sanctifying: I am called to "make holy" the places and spaces in which I find myself. This includes my family, my social circles, my workplace, my community, and the larger society. I can do this by committing to carrying the light of Christ into every situation.

Prophet/teaching and preaching: Prophets speak on God's behalf. They watch and listen for God in our world and point it out to others. They teach others about how God is moving and doing something new. I can do this by accompanying others on their faith journeys and helping them discern God's presence in their own lives. I do not need to be employed by the Church to do this. In fact, I observe as hundreds of volunteers and ministry leaders in my parish community do this week after week!

King/governing: Governing from a place of servant leadership means assuring that everyone has what they need to grow into the person God created them to be. I can be an advocate for justice, I can help make connections and use my network to serve others, I can contribute in a personal way by accompanying people with the support and care they need.

Jennifer's proclamation resonates with Pope Francis's teaching in *Evangelium Gaudium*:

> In all the baptized, from first to last, the sanctifying power of the Spirit is at work, impelling us to evangelize. In virtue of their baptism, all the members of the People of God have become missionary disciples. All the baptized, whatever their position in the Church or their level of instruction in the faith, are agents of evangelization, and it would be insufficient to envisage a plan of evangelization to be carried out by professionals while the rest of the faithful would simply be passive recipients. (nos. 119–20)

It is worth noting a point made by Kerry Weber: "People also assume that women in leadership in the church must feel constant resentment about the roles they cannot hold. But I have found these women to be tremendously joyful people, even when faced with injustices within the church. It is their deep belief in the joy of the gospel that compels them to gladly labor in the vineyards of the church and to work against injustice and prejudice on all fronts."[14]

As the leadership of lay people emanates from their baptism, the task ahead as Pope Francis states is how to enable this leadership without clericalizing them. On this challenge, John Cavadini directs our attention to "co-responsibility" as the antidote to clericalizing the laity.[15] Cavadini draws heavily

---

[14] Kerry Weber, response to Carolyn Woo questionnaire, March 22, 2021.

[15] John Cavadini, "Co-Responsibility: An Antidote to Clericalizing the Laity?" *Church Life Journal* (March 26, 2020).

from Pope Benedict, who observes that the vision of co-responsibility from the Second Vatican Council has not yet been fully implemented.

> At the same time, it should be recognized that the re-awakening of spiritual and pastoral energies that has been happening in recent years has not always produced the desired growth and development. . . . This fact tells us that the luminous pages which the Council dedicated to the laity were not yet sufficiently adapted to or impressed on the minds of Catholics or in pastoral procedures. On the one hand there is still a tendency to identify the Church unilaterally with the hierarchy, forgetting the common responsibility, the common mission of the People of God, which, in Christ we all share. . . . To what extent is the pastoral co-responsibility of all, and particularly of the laity, recognized and encouraged?[16]

In Cavadini's words, "Where are the lay leaders in the mission of the Church, the lay-led projects, the lay-led initiatives?"[17]

Continuing on changes needed to achieve co-responsibility, Benedict advises:

> It is necessary to improve pastoral structures in such a way that the co-responsibility of all the members of the People of God in their entirety is gradually promoted, with respect for vocations and for the respective roles of the consecrated and of lay people. This demands a change in mindset, particularly concerning lay people. They must no

---

[16] "Address of His Holiness Pope Benedict XVI at the Opening of the Pastoral Convention of the Diocese of Rome on the Theme 'Church Membership and Pastoral Co-Responsibility,'" Basilica of Saint John Lateran, May 26, 2009.

[17] Cavadini, "Co-Responsibility."

longer be viewed as "collaborators" of the clergy but truly recognized as "co-responsible," for the Church's being and action, thereby fostering the consolidation of a mature and committed laity.[18]

In a speech in 2012, Pope Benedict further elaborated on the fruits of co-responsibility:

Many benefits for the Church are to be expected from this familiar relationship between the laity and the pastors. The sense of their own responsibility is strengthened in the laity, their zeal is encouraged, they are more ready to unite their energies to the work of their pastors. The latter, helped by the experience of the laity, are in a position to judge more clearly and more appropriately in spiritual as well as in temporal matters. Strengthened by all her members, the Church can thus more effectively fulfill her mission for the life of the world. . . . In this phase of history, in the light of the Church's social Magisterium also strive to be, increasingly, a laboratory of the "globalization of solidarity and charity," so as to grow, with the whole Church, in the co-responsibility of offering humanity a future of hope and with the courage to formulate demanding proposals.[19]

The above teachings unequivocally summon lay people to join with ordained clergy not just to collaborate with each other, but to take up co-responsibility in bringing Christ's light into the world with vigor and renewed energies. The pontiffs

---

[18] "Address of His Holiness Pope Benedict XVI," May 26, 2009.

[19] "Message of His Holiness Pope Benedict XVI on the Occasion of the Sixth Ordinary Assembly of the International Forum of Catholic Action," August 10, 2012.

declare that, while differing in essence but not in degree with the clergy, the leadership of lay people must be cultivated, and in a way that does not clericalize them. There is honest admission that the mandate about the laity has not been put into practice to the extent envisioned by Vatican II.

What we should take away with respect to women's leadership is not so much the absence of recognition, advocacy, and formal teaching. The obstacle lies in the lack of change. Inertia is fed by feeble challenges to current structures and the passive foot dragging that cripples substantive action behind intentions. A lack of knowledge and experience may slow down progress. Naming the problem, though, is the first step in solving it.

Misperception 4: Women Are Not Well-Suited for Leadership Roles in Catholic Ministries

The contributors herein also point to attitudes that they have encountered or observed relating to women leading in the Church. Some people feel that women's greatest contribution should be in the home as spouse and parent, and not as professional staff. Their roles are most appropriate as volunteers or support staff providing supplementary assistance. Women are "worker bees," not meant to lead. Do they have the requisite skills, experiences, temperament to make difficult decisions? Will they be too emotional? Accustomed to small projects, can women be trusted to formulate strategic direction? Exercise financial judgment and discipline? Will women be able to hold their own in debates and discussions? Will they speak their mind in a group of men? Are women even interested?

These stereotypes and lack of confidence have come from women as well as men. Women have spoken of their doubts when they or their friends receive invitations to serve in some type of leadership capacity. Certainly the difficulties cited above are real for some people. But they are not gender based. I contend much of the deficit when this exists is due to lack of opportunity, exposure, and practice. To the extent that women have had fewer occasions to serve on governance or advisory boards or have a place at the table where decisions are being made, these doubts will linger. Women's skills and experiences will grow when they are invited, supported, engaged, and mentored.

2

Attributes of Women Leaders in This Book

"I never set out to become a 'leader' in the church," said Ann
Manion, who serves as the president of the Women's Care Center, the largest network of agencies in the United States that
counsel and support pregnant women to continue with their
pregnancies to full term.

What is organizational leadership? From the Webster dictionary to the myriad of studies on leadership, there are easily
as many definitions as authors who have written on the topic.
Theories have been proposed and debunked on the traits, styles,
personalities, skills, and approaches of effective leaders. Most
would agree that the "how" to effective leadership is contingent
on the challenges and contexts faced by leaders. There is not a
single blueprint for leading.

Despite these qualifiers, the literature does yield some degree
of convergence on what constitutes organizational leadership.
For the purpose of this book, let me define *organizational leadership* as "the capacity to mobilize people and resources to achieve
constructive outcomes toward mission."

Leadership is not self-focused even though some people at
the top are. The necessary marker of leadership is when someone
else, specifically those our mission claims to serve, are better off

because of the organization's efforts. Organizational leadership is not a solo venture as in the work of a craftsman, philosopher, scholar, scientist, or artist, however much these have enriched our aesthetics, culture, insights, knowledge, and well being. It operates through a collection of people and requires fostering relationships, through both formal structures and culture, toward coherence, collaboration, and mutuality.

While healthy relationships are necessary, they are not sufficient to deliver effective outcomes and probably not sustainable over the long term unless members of the organization are properly supported by resources, systems, clarity of purpose and direction, and some capacity for organizational self-correction and adaptation.

For Catholic ministries, as Pope Benedict XVI emphasizes in his 2006 *Deus Caritas Est,* we need something more. The charitable activities of the church must be distinguished by a mark beyond the requisite effectiveness and professionalism. These must not become just another form of social assistance.

> We are dealing with human beings, and human beings always need something more than technically proper care. They need humanity. They need heartfelt concern. They who work for the Church's charitable organizations must be distinguished by the fact that they do not merely meet the needs of the moment, but they dedicate themselves to others with heartfelt concerns, enabling them to experience the richness of their humanity they need to be led to that encounter with God in Christ which awakens their love and opens their spirits to others. (no. 31)

For the women leaders featured in this book, this deep love for God and neighbor is unquestionably the compass by which they find their way. While their tapestries of service may present different pictures, they are woven with a common spirit. Let me highlight five aspects of this spirit.

They Are Compelled to Serve Those in Need

In *Fratelli Tutti*, Pope Francis's 2020 letter, he employs the parable of the Good Samaritan to make his points about brotherhood and social friendship. At the encounter with a stranger brutalized and near death, is our concern for ourselves or for the other?

In their essays the women leaders implicitly or explicitly describe the pull of service to others. The desire to help others starts early for some. For Sr. Simone, even before the age of two, she took to heart her father's daily parting words to take care of her mother and younger sister. By third grade, sensing that it was wrong for the teacher to ignore certain students, she created a play that included the entire class.

Ana Ventura Phares's career moves are imprinted with her father's gentle summons to look out for farmworkers and those at the margin who have few advocates.

"Leaders bring their gifts to wherever they're called to service, and help others develop and exercise their gifts in service to the gospel as well." This statement from Kim Daniels runs through her different engagements for religious freedom and pro-life advocacy through legal work, communication, and policy discussion.

The orientation to serve others is beautifully captured by Sr. Simone as "walk willing." This is to move toward the needs of others and into places of suffering. It is the capacity to see and not turn away and, like the Good Samaritan, to subordinate one's own plans, agenda, biases, and fears for a greater need. It is the death of self, in small and daily encounters as much as in big leaps of faith, for the other. And on the other side of this death is resurrection: an encounter with God and a new beginning for both the one who gives and the one who receives.

At Catholic Relief Services (CRS) the focus on the other is a rallying force that unites over five thousand colleagues with diverse backgrounds spanning over a hundred countries and even more cultures. CRS adopts Catholic social teachings as its operating guidelines, with the mission to serve all people on the basis of need, not creed. Across the different religions of our staff—Christian, Hindu, Muslim, Buddhist, and other—everyone embraces these teachings as Catholic inspired and universally applicable. The focus on beneficiaries to meet their needs as whole people, safeguard their dignity, engage them as equals, and strengthen their capacity as communities is our common compass and the touchstone by which we make decisions. It is the calculus by which we set priorities and arbitrate differences. That we exist for "the other" also becomes the social contract between colleagues and partners. It is the glue that binds us all.

One anecdote relates to how I learned about the real value of money after a full career as a business school professor and dean. A good first cup of coffee would kick start my day. When I first joined CRS, we had non-dairy creamers that coagulated into clumps in my coffee. Half serious, I asked whether we could afford real creamer. The answer was, "Yes, we could, but five dollars will feed a family of four for a week in the countries we serve."

What an important lesson for the new CEO! From this creamer example, through all decisions big and small, stewardship of resources is filtered through the reality of and in solidarity with the people whose care God entrusted to us. This commitment to the people being served enables CRS to maintain one of the lowest administrative expense ratios: 8–9 percent year after year.

Deep affinity for the people we serve can lead to uncommon results. At a meeting on malaria treatment whereby a very admirable percentage of the target population had been reached, congratulations were being offered. At this point a colleague interrupted: "What about the others? Do they not count? Are we giving ourselves permission to walk away?"

Similarly at the business college at Notre Dame, the team was quite pleased with the job placement result of 90 percent for the graduating class. It would place us in the top tier of our peers. Frowning in the midst of mild euphoria, one colleague drew our attention to the 10 percent or seventy students who were still empty handed. Do they count? What do they need from us? The fact that these students have not succeeded yet means they need more help, greater attention from us, not dismissiveness.

A deep love for the people we serve would raise questions such as these: Are they getting our best efforts and ideas? Is the problem really solved, or did we just offer a bandaid? Did we leave behind the weaker ones? Can we go farther? Where can we look to learn more? Are we worthy of the privilege of serving them?

Love just doesn't quit.

They Are Committed to Their Staff

Not surprisingly, the impulse to serve people in need also expresses itself in the care for colleagues. The leaders featured here are exemplary in the emphasis they place on developing their people, acknowledging their contributions, and building their sense of belonging.

Cyril Cruz understands her position of principal as serving the teachers whom she notes as the "backbone" of the school. Her job is to support them toward their success.

Julie Sullivan defines leadership as

> commitment to serve and to prioritize the organization and its people over oneself. The leader's guiding principle for decision-making must be what best serves the common good of the organization and its people. Leadership is about

compelling a community of people to want to follow a common goal with you. US Supreme Court Justice Ruth Ginsberg said, 'Fight for the things that you care about, but do it in a way that will lead others to join you.' People follow effective leaders because they want to, rather than because they feel they have to.

In faith-based ministries my experience is that colleagues are best served and inspired by mission and purpose. The leadership "pull" derives foremost from mission before personality, power, or resources. It draws people from the heart, thus honoring their passion and values and dignifying them as whole people. Mission invites colleagues to be part of something bigger than a job. It is the calculus to which every member of the organization, regardless of rank and level, has access.

Effective leaders recognize that mission is the raison d'être that constitutes the common purpose of the organization. Our leaders work hard to engage others to give it life and relevance, integrate it in big and small decisions. Most important, they model this behavior so as to become both messenger and message. These leaders carefully cultivate a culture and approach whereby mission becomes the compass, tuning fork, and drumbeat.

As Annemarie Reilly reflects, "Leadership is about mobilizing people to achieve a shared goal or result. I am personally most inspired as a leader when tapping into the why behind the work. It makes mobilizing people much easier when we have such mission-focused work and Catholic social teaching guiding us."

Many of the women leaders in this book express the desire to see colleagues develop their talents, push back the boundaries they have set for themselves, and support them in the process. "One major responsibility of a leader is to be alert to developing talented people into various leadership roles," Sr. Carol Keehan writes. She emphasizes the need to use the "talents and competencies of all members. . . . The successful leader brings out the best in individuals and teams, not just in technical skills, but in their humanity, 'the better angels we all have.' It means having a deep sense of the dignity of each person and the contributions they make and the needs and aspirations they have."

I am particularly grateful for a piece of advice from Sr. Carol, whose attentiveness to her staff leads me to be more mindful of a bad practice many of us fall into:

> I loved living and working in the hospital but I had to make myself very conscious of the fact that when I was walking around I could not take the time to think about issues, I had to be tuned to the people I was walking past. I owed it to them to smile, speak, and chat a bit. Walking around deep in thought is often so misunderstood. Staff may only see you once every six weeks and you walk by without saying hello or thanks. But if you did stop and ask about a family member, comment on the compliment about them you received, and so on, you have made their month. It is important to realize that you are not walking through an automated factory.

Berni Neal, a member of different boards, sees her role not so much as being in charge, but taking care of those who are in charge. She suggests that "when things go right, you give away the credits. And when they go wrong, you take responsibility."

I learned an important lesson in the last month of my tenure at CRS. By then, I had a bit of time on my hands, and I offered to buy lunch for any colleague who would take me up on it. It was a chance for me to get together with many folks I had not worked with directly or had not gotten to know well.

I invited my colleagues to tell me about themselves, what they wanted me to know about them. I became fully engrossed in these stories. One told me how she raised two nieces when her sister could not; another talked about the loss of his wife and how hard it was to venture into new things; one staff member proudly shared his gift for singing and the many overseas tours he had done. Each spoke of what CRS meant to them, their proudest achievements, and their vision for the ministry. Many also shared how difficult it was for them and the fears they had when I first came in as CEO, an outsider with a mandate to review and reposition CRS for the future.

What I learned was not that change is unsettling for people. I had been on both sides of change, so I understood the fears. But the tremors are amplified when colleagues feel that the people applying the red pens to the organizational chart do not know them or their expertise, do not have a sense of their history with the organization, or do not understand their deep commitment to making a new direction work. They become faceless and a number to be placed on the separation list.

The need to be known is universal and cuts across all levels and functions. I can easily point to a calendar that left no room for these "nonbusiness" meetings. Looking back, I could have made at least an hour available each week for such exchanges. I was wrong to think that this is not important work!

Pope Francis calls for us to engage one another. Engagement requires meeting in person: looking into the face of the other where life stories are carved, listening to the words of the heart, sharing something about ourselves, and caring about the other person. Attention, as Simone Weil writes, is prayer. Willingness to spend time with another is the currency of good relationships without which organizations cannot function effectively. For people to care about the organization, they need to know that the organization cares about them.

So often in administration and in leadership we are "trained" not to let personal aspects get into the picture. We are to maintain distance and space so that we can "pull the trigger" and not let emotions cloud our judgment. Yet who would trust a leader who makes decisions without empathy?

Leadership is difficult for many different reasons: making the right strategic choices, getting resources, implementing correctly, and communicating with clarity and encouragement. But the most difficult part, I think, rests on accepting the responsibility for how decisions affect colleagues. What do leaders owe the people who could lose their livelihoods, career momentum, sense of worth, and peace of mind because of our choices. Real leadership may call for losing sleep over people issues. People-focused leadership is, by definition, personal.

They Take Ownership of Problems

Another inspiring aspect is how the women take on problems and challenges. They tackle problems with creativity, efforts, and adaptability. Job descriptions, for these leaders, do not set the finish line for where they stop. Instead, they embrace these as invitations to take the organization to its fullest potential in service of its mission.

I think this is very much like motherhood. Mothers do not operate within a job description while they assume responsibility for their children. When a child has a problem, mom does not stop with the first expert in town when the issue persists. She branches out to seek alternative opinions from different specialists located near or far, and she reaches beyond what she knows to seek resolution. Her comfort zone expands to accommodate her search.

It is instructive to learn from the examples shared by Betsy Bohlen, the chief operating officer of a large archdiocese. The diocesan staff were intent on implementing a decision the archbishop had made although they were aware that he did not have full information. In such situations, which are rather common in organizations, it is often "safer" to just soldier on and not "rock the boat." Instead, Betsy urged them to go back to the archbishop presenting all the facts that were relevant to the case.

The archbishop responded with, "If I knew those facts, I never would have made that original decision."

Similarly when the staff wanted the pastors to do more on financial management, Betsy challenged them to provide the tools and information that could make the tasks more manageable. So the staff took extra steps to provide informative summaries of the parishes, recommendations for actions, steps to be taken, and means for tracking. Desired change followed.

Betsy sums up: "I believe, ultimately, that one exercises leadership best by assuming individual ownership for a full problem regardless of actual role, rather than stopping short based on a perceived limit to one's role or authority. This approach is almost always appreciated by more senior leaders: they appreciate the initiative taking, thought partnership, and support from someone who is helping to co-own a problem."

In the context of board governance we similarly find Karen Rauenhorst following a problem to its logical conclusion. It is not uncommon in board meetings for members to keep silent, even when it is clear that the board has not gotten to the bottom of an issue. Board members sometimes dread and avoid raising points that may be awkward. They stop short of achieving sufficient clarity and coherence for implementation. As Karen describes, "I tend to ask the questions of management that many board members did not want to ask."

To get a sense of what people are concerned about, Karen as board chair would reach out to the members individually ahead of meetings to solicit their thoughts and advice. She cited an example of a CEO who had not heeded the board's call for strategic change for three years. Upon some probing of fellow members, who were mostly men, she found that they were keenly aware of the problem but were unwilling to "upset the apple cart." Karen reflects, "I do feel women leaders do their research on specific topics and will many times ask the tough questions that are swirling around the room."

Going the extra mile calls for additional work, taking risks, not settling for tried-and-true solutions if these do not go far enough to address problems. It goes back to the first attribute of emphasizing others' well being over our own discomfort and perceived limits.

They Seek to Heal and Bridge Differences

I once served on the board of the Center for Creative Leadership, the preeminent leadership development institute founded over fifty years ago. One key trend it identified in its research was the importance of moving across groups or "boundary-spanning" leadership in addition to the more commonly understood mode of "within-group" leadership. Given the functional complexity of problems, different stakeholders involved, and conflicting points of view, leadership requires engaging constructively and fruitfully across differences.

We are at a moment in this country when cultural and political polarization has significantly stymied progress toward enacting legislation through bipartisan give and take. A poll conducted in April 2021[1] reports that about 70 percent of Americans believe that they have more in common than reflected in media, but 44 percent see greater difficulties in dealing with disagreements.

Even within the Catholic Church we see unfortunate divisive tactics that amplify differences and rigid labeling that vilifies people with different priorities. Public attacks and name calling are sometimes used as fodder to drive subscription to various media enterprises and sustain donations. The underlying business models rely on half-truths to further distort positions, damage reputation, and create sensationalism.

---

[1] Public Agenda/USA TODAY, "Overcoming Divisiveness," Hidden Common Ground survey, April 27, 2021.

Of this societal disintegration Sr. Donna observes, "In some metaphorical way, we are globally facing the terror of an unwelcome oncoming train that is being powered by the energy of hatred and self-serving judgmentalism and fear."

Against this context, I note the spirit of communio reflected by some of our women leaders. They call for building bridges and fostering understanding. For example, Sr. Donna completes her comment above with an affirmation:

> And we intuitively realize that the only way we are going to avert further disaster is if we take action on behalf of the other. . . . Another way of saying this is that universal communion, living in deliberate relatedness, must outweigh any intent we have of overpowering the different other in order to protect our own comforts. . . . I believe that one of most crucial skills wise leaders must learn and undertake is to promote the healing of the ruptures that surround us on all sides. This reconciling behavior necessitates our taking an entirely different approach toward dealing with conflicts, differences, and dissension.

Recognizing that urban and rural populations hold vastly different opinions, Sr. Simone approached this potentially divisive dynamic by convening five "Dialogues across Geographic Divides" before the 2020 election. Participants from both cities and rural communities shared their lived experiences, enabling a better appreciation of both their commonalities and their divergent perspectives. More important, such dialogues reveal the whys behind the differences. Understanding cultivates empathy and invites creativity for crafting mutually beneficial resolutions.

Kim Daniels, calling for leaders to engage others with different points of view where possible and challenging these when necessary, does so by convening forums on different issues. These sessions foster listening based on genuine respect for the other.

At the same time, such civil engagement also enables a dignified space to discuss, probe, and honor differences.

The work of CRS often entails rebuilding livelihoods and fortifying community development after deadly conflicts or amid longstanding grievances. Reconciliation is a precondition to make room for collaboration, shared progress, and protection of rights to ensure peaceful coexistence.

Efforts at healing have brought together neighbors who once destroyed one another's families: Rwandans whose relatives died by the hand of the other, or Palestinian and Jewish parents who lost children in their deadly skirmishes. I have observed the grace of Cambodians who place their priority on building a peaceful society for their children rather than seeking vengeance and retribution for their own suffering. Many women do the work and provide the spirit behind these efforts for peacebuilding. This work entails binding wounds, recreating bonds within a community that has been dispersed, and reaching out to other groups. Such healing is fostered by acceptance for all people as one family in God. I am inspired to see this capacity in the leaders featured in this book.

Their Work Is Rooted in Faith

Behind the vision, care for others, and tenacity of the women leaders is their unshakable faith in God. Many of them were raised by parents who modeled their faith through piety and service to the community. Sr. Simone and Ana Phares saw their parents living out their faith by standing with and for people in need. That became their work.

Berni Neal fell in love with St. Bernadette, her patron saint, and the Blessed Mother at a young age. She felt special and comforted by their love for her. From a child's simple understanding, she grew in devotion that led to the enthusiastic "yes" to the many ministries of the church that reached out for her leadership.

Disposed to open her heart from her faith, Berni would step up over and over again, noting, "I fell in love with their mission, I fell in love with their team. I signed up."

Marian spirituality also informs the ideal leadership approach held by Kerry Weber. She turns to Mary as an "example of quiet leadership. . . . She [Mary] thinks deeply about her decisions and is a woman of her word and a team player ('May it be done to me according to your word.') She is good at delegating and encouraging others in their own ministry ('Do whatever he tells you.') She celebrates and lifts up other women (Hi, Elizabeth!), and she is a humble servant."

The faith that drives these leaders' work also infuses their family lives. Cyril Cruz locates her vocation as a principal in conjunction with her dedication to her family. To her, it is not a choice between work and family but the simultaneous flourishing of both.

Jennifer Fiduccia sees her leadership playing out not only in her pastoral work but at home. She recognizes that she is modeling for her four children, particularly her two daughters, what it means to grow into the woman God calls her to be.

Leaders have to make difficult decisions such as balancing competing needs of colleagues, beneficiaries, the local community, and the organization itself. Decisions have to be made in the context of incomplete information with aspects of the future rendered as best guesses. Success of actions taken, best bets, is driven by various forces not all within the control of the leader. Just think about the upheaval created by the COVID-19 pandemic. Imagine the responsibilities of Catholic school principals trying to manage through enrollment declines. In addition, leaders are vulnerable to criticism from stakeholders, for handling crises for which they have no experience, or for results that fall short of goals.

A leader could simply be weighed down, stressed out, or habitually anxious. Cyril Cruz, principal of a Catholic school, operates at the nexus of all the forces mentioned above: making budget, achieving enrollment targets, meeting different needs of the student body, and keeping school in session during the pandemic. However, instead of being laden down with the burden of what will go awry, Cruz moves forward with equanimity, trusting that "God will guide us in the sacred duty of forming souls." She relies on mass, daily family rosary, and weekly confessions as the foundation for navigating challenges. Knowledge that she is held in God's palm confers a certain confidence, calm, and the peace of mind that Julian of Norwich counsels, "All shall be well, all manner of things shall be well."

By nature, I am a worrywart. My modus operandi is to put more items on my to-do list and organize my tasks so that the "enemy" is in view. The fallback position: put in more hours. But through the decades, by divine grace, the most profound lesson I have learned is that everything really does not depend on me. God has always been here. Actually, the more vexing my situation, the more I have grown in faith, as these are the times when God's fingerprints are most discernible.

Within the first week of my arrival at the University of Notre Dame, legendary President-Emeritus Fr. Theodore "Ted" Hesburgh asked to see me. His intent was to extend a warm personal welcome into his family. As an elder of a tribe would do, he wanted me to know what this family stands for and what we live by. Two pieces of advice from Fr. Ted to hold dear: "Mediocrity is not the way to serve the Blessed Mother," and "At all times, just pray, 'Come, Holy Spirit.'"

In my correspondence at Notre Dame and later at CRS, I signed off with "Yours in Notre Dame" and "Yours in Christ," respectively. Each time I did so, I was conscious of the privilege of working in their holy names and tried to be mindful of the responsibilities of bearing witness to their presence.

Every morning I would start my workday either at the Grotto at Notre Dame or in the CRS chapel. I would recount to the

Father, Son, Holy Spirit, and Blessed Mother what transpired the day before and what lay ahead that day. I felt as if I was at God's kitchen table, where families gather and go through both major and mundane happenings. I would remind the Trinity and the Blessed Mother that we all have to show up in the office as it is a workday.

"Come, Holy Spirit" was never far from my lips. On the days when something particularly challenging intimidated me, I would set an extra chair for the Holy Spirit. I realize that when we lead with the Holy Spirit, we set our focus on what our beneficiaries need rather than what we can do within current capabilities and resources. A gap opens up: an invitation from the Spirit to stretch beyond ourselves for the service of others.

Our work is not merely labor or even service, but the expression of our gifts in gratitude to God, with God, and in God. After serving on an interim basis, Ana Ventura Phares was elated to step into the executive director position of the Catholic Charities in Monterrey. She notes, "I found that I loved the work because it was all my past positions rolled into one incredible job with Jesus in the middle!"

3

Challenges

Co-Responsibility: Still Early in the Journey

The challenges of women leading in Catholic ministries seem most frequent and difficult in parish settings. Women account for three out of four ecclesial lay ministers who lead pastoral ministries, youth ministries, liturgical ministries, social outreach, and RCIA (the Rite of Christian Initiation of Adults). Yet the experiences many described are contrary to hospitality, acceptance, and respect.

Operating in environments of different degrees of clericalism and sexism, female ecclesial lay ministers describe hurtful experiences of being sidelined, in ways gratuitous or patronizing, for not knowing their theology or their place. The women felt they were treated as threats or imposters when they disagreed with the clergy. They were maybe politely tolerated but not taken seriously, and certainly not engaged as equals in faith and in intellect.

Women recalled decisions being made without meaningful consultation with the individuals involved. Some women were simply not at the table and heard about the change from other sources. *Forgotten, invisible,* and *insignificant* are some of the adjectives they offer. They described their sense of vulnerability when programs were terminated with the arrival of a new pastor.

They did not know whether their positions would be next in line for cuts.

Sexism plays out in the higher titles, larger scope of authority, and greater deference that male colleagues enjoy. Women are sometimes expected to pick up the loose ends, absorb the extra load, overlook sharp or insensitive remarks, and be the cultural caretakers of the work team. For the sake of maintaining harmonious relations, women are to brush these off as being a "good team member" and "men being men."

Such expectations lock women into gender roles and downplay the professional treatment due them. They foster an asymmetry that prevents growth for both men and women by tolerating bias and creating inequity. In certain settings pastors may be more comfortable with men and maintain social rapport that flows into work matters. Some women found that they have to go through male colleagues who have the pastor's ear to advocate for their projects.

There is also the thorny issue of the long-term viability of professional employment within the church. Many positions require graduate credentials, imposing expenses on top of undergraduate loans. These financial burdens frequently cannot be accommodated by the salaries of full-time and part-time positions offered by the church. The advantage of free education to seminarians cannot be overestimated, and the absence of this for women would continue to hinder their participation. One woman lamented how she could not afford Catholic education for her children when that was the most powerful formation experience for her.

Compounding this financial burden is when women, "the second income," are paid less than their male peers. This practice ignores the reality that some women are the single or primary breadwinner shouldering major expenses. These women have to plan for their children's future educational needs and their own retirement. At risk is the long-term retention of these women.

It is concerning when women ministry leaders indicate that their work is seen primarily as support for ordained clergy and less as a manifestation of their own baptismal call. Many recognize that they serve only by permission of the hierarchy, who hold pastoral authority over them. It is important that women's gifts and their vocations be valued and promoted on their own merits, and not on the basis of utility and as complements to the work of the clergy.

Clearly the co-responsibility called for by Pope Benedict XVI unfolds unequally in practice. Co-responsibility is not simply off-loading unwanted responsibilities or tasks. It is not reaching down to a subordinate, but a raising up of a partner and equal to make God's love palpable in the world. Pastors demonstrate different enthusiasm and proclivity for the level of co-ministering where lay people "must no longer be viewed as 'collaborators' of the clergy but truly recognized as 'co-responsible' for the Church's being and action, thereby fostering the consolidation of a mature and committed laity."[1]

Women as Outsiders

Ministries outside of parish structures such as Catholic health systems, social services, universities, and media are more likely to operate under governance structures that are not dependent on one individual. These tend to provide clear definitions of responsibilities and decision-making authority as well as proper channels for accountability. Women leaders in these institutions are less likely to face overt putdowns, casual dismissals, or blatant inequality compared to male colleagues. They face a different set of challenges.

---

[1] "Address of His Holiness Pope Benedict XVI at the Opening of the Pastoral Convention of the Diocese of Rome on the Theme 'Church Membership and Pastoral Co-Responsibility,'" Basilica of Saint John Lateran, May 26, 2009.

Women who run large ministries are likely to be the first females in these roles. Whether recruited from the outside or from the ministry, they are not a part of the clerical hierarchy. Women are outsiders to this structure. Most clergy have simply not worked with women as peers or for women as superiors. Women executives are still oddities in some situations.

Upon joining CRS, I attended my first meeting on refugee assistance where senior church leaders had assembled in Rome from all over the world. CRS had an extensive portfolio of programs covering over a hundred countries and serving over a hundred million people. I was told much work would get done over breaks and social gatherings in informal exchanges. Different bishops would want to get a sense of continued funding. I should expect suggestions for new programs or expanded coverage. Some would have questions on work progress and emerging challenges. For my prep, I stayed up late in the fog of jet lag to be ready for these conversations.

At the meeting, after introducing myself to different leaders, no such conversations ensued. I was asked mostly about my flight and my new role, but nothing else. No big talk, not even much small talk. I tried to provide a few leads into the business issues, but no takers. With bewilderment and slight panic, I realized that these leaders were not comfortable broaching their needs with me.

At that point I recalled that men's networks have a certain code of communication, a way of asking for favors or letting their preferences be known without actually asking. Important issues are presented under the cloak of jokes or understatements. Messages are sent through seemingly inconsequential banter. Clearly I was not a part of this network yet. Gender was a factor but so was the lack of interaction. It was my first encounter with the bishops and theirs with me. Good conversations rely on mutual understanding and trust built from years of interaction. I had none of this.

I presumed that moving forward on the refugee programs was as important to them as to me. I knew what I had to do: enlist my chief operating officer, Sean Callahan, who had thirty years of history at CRS and great relationships with the bishops. It would work better if he stepped in and started the banter. The conversations flowed.

To be fair, the discomfort of men engaging women as leaders is not unique to the Catholic Church. It is endemic in many cultures and rural communities CRS serves: men sit in the front and speak; women and children sit in the back or to the side and stay silent. As I visited these communities, I never pushed the issue. I was happy to be placed with the women of the village, from whom I learned an immense amount about their reality, ingenuity, and needs.

Our staff would communicate that the purpose of my visit was to learn from the leaders how we could serve their community better. I wanted to know their dreams for their children. More often than not, they invited me in and offered up the best from their stock of grains and livestock. Eventually the fact that I am a woman receded into the background. Sitting cross-legged with them, I became a friend and partner bearing good will.

Young women have often shared the experience of being shut out when working in the church. One could bristle. Or one could choose to understand that long-established practices take time and space to change, and change comes in small steps; to recognize that our mission is not to force a lesson on women's equality, but to serve the communities in our care. Gender divides can be bridged, but this takes patience, understanding, and respect. One of the women leaders in this book observes with humor that while there may be receptivity to a woman leader, there is discomfort in having too many senior women at one time. The important lesson is to not assume the worst of people, and not to equate unfamiliarity and lack of practice with unwillingness. A chip on the shoulder can prematurely foreclose paths of mutual understanding and collaboration.

Clearly, not every cleric would change even with time and interaction to welcome women as key players and equals. There are clergy who treat women in condescending ways not out of practice, but out of competitiveness and insecurity. We may chalk this up to clericalism, but such behavior exists in secular organizations also. In such cases one should minimize engagement, avoid overpaying in the way of emotional preoccupation, safeguard against lashing out from hurt or from our own insecurity, and refrain from reacting with the smallest version of ourselves.

Many Catholic ministries are steeped in protocols and norms derived from canon law, doctrinal guidelines, social teachings, and past practices. Leaders recruited from the outside have to discover these over time. In every organization there are "red lines" that demarcate the scope of acceptable questions for the group. For example, in some organizations one may raise concerns about nonperforming programs, but not the people behind these. In other contexts certain programs are "protected" for a host of reasons and are not up for assessment. Some boards take up succession as a priority, while others shy away from the issue altogether. It is necessary to locate the red lines without the benefit of clearly marked boundaries or brightly lit signs that read "no entry."

I once served on a diocesan finance committee. A budget requisition indicated that insurance premiums had gone up substantially. The problem of sexual abuse by clergy was emerging nationally, and insurance companies adjusted their pricing for this risk. It seemed to me that this was not merely a budget issue but had more serious implications. I raised my hand and posed what seemed to me a logical question, "Are there similar abuse cases in our diocese?" The answer to me was gentle but firm, "Carolyn, this is a matter for the brother priests." The discussion went no further and we approved the budget.

Trying new approaches, looking at problems in new ways, incorporating new priorities, and meeting new challenges will eventually get us close to the red lines. In the decades that followed that exchange, I would ask my older self how I should have responded. Should I have put a toe beyond the red line? Does the context allow for constructive listening and reflection? Could I find another context to raise the issue privately? And how are we to grow together into a better community if each of us just steps back behind the red line?

Women often begin "out of network" without a strong sense of belonging. The experience of not belonging is endemic to many women who have finally gained entry. They do not have the same experiences; they are not part of the same social networks; they have no golf or fish stories to share or ready jokes to break the ice. The feeling of not belonging is of natural interest to me: a Chinese immigrant woman whose background, affiliations, and experiences seldom intersect with anybody else's.

Over the years I have come to the conclusion that belonging is overrated. To my chagrin, I find that everyone feels some sense of not belonging, even men or the most "in" person in the "in" group. With the move toward diversity I realize that we are invited not for how much we are like the others but for what we bring to the table that is uniquely ours.

Our contribution is to add perspectives that enhance decision making for the good of the organization. Preparation, focus on the issues, clear thinking, and crisp articulation are the currency for participation. Having spoken one's truth for the benefit of the problem, refrain from looking for affirmation or agreement. Being an outsider is integral to personal and professional growth as we venture beyond the known and familiar.

Negotiating Differences

It should be expected that clergy and their lay collaborators do not always have the same priorities. Friction can develop from these differences. At a formal dinner I was seated next to a cardinal, and at some point we were the only two people left at the table. With genuine interest he asked me about my challenges leading the US church's global humanitarian ministry. There were many "safe" topics that I could talk about, but I decided to raise a vexing issue involving the church.

A diocese in Africa had raised an objection to one of our long-standing practices. CRS has extensive programming across Africa. The programs cover many areas of work including childhood nutrition and development, education, agricultural livelihoods, health and well being, HIV/AIDS interventions, and peacebuilding. The grievance was that CRS does not engage in preferential hiring of Catholics in the diocese, and some program leadership positions have gone to people of other faiths. Ill feelings were developing.

CRS's mission is to serve on the basis of need, never on the basis of creed. We are to serve all people. A mirror policy is adopted for the recruitment of colleagues. One pillar of the CRS operating guidelines is to build up local capacity and develop local leaders in accordance with the principle of subsidiarity. We do so by hiring the best local talent. Preferential hiring based on faith contradicts our mission and guidelines. It can also undermine trust and collegiality in regions where religious relations are fragile. I felt my choice was to compromise on a CRS principle to keep peace or to create ill will with the local church.

The cardinal affirmed that I should not bend a principle that is integral to what CRS stands for. But he also wanted me to see the problem through another lens, not my implicit interpretation of church hierarchy coming down on me. He explained that the Catholic Church in many parts of Africa is the minority church.

It does not have many resources and has to negotiate sensitive political and cultural currents. CRS is akin to a rich and influential cousin from America who can give it a boost, a public acknowledgment of kinship, and an unambiguous show of solidarity. The church would benefit from the reputational purchase and elevated social standing that comes with such a relationship. We are its family, and our seeming disregard can be humiliating.

I got it. This is the age-old inviolable social doctrine of "saving face" that governs all relationships and interactions in Chinese culture. It is an alternative to the "power-domination," "lay vs. clergy," or "win vs. loss" thinking that populates Western thinking. How could I have forgotten this?

With this new frame I found an entire universe of possible options to lift up our local church partners. We can publicize our partnership, hold joint briefings of the objectives and accomplishments of the projects, shine the spotlight on them. We can share our human resource plan with the local diocese to give early notice on the attributes and skills we are looking for in upcoming projects. In appropriate situations when the local church is ready, we have invited it to serve as principal of proposed grants, and CRS to offer support as its technical partner. We can also offer the local Catholic ministries organizational assessments that allow them to identify areas for accompaniment, training, and development.

Not surprising, many times CRS has to say no to the myriad requests that come from the local church. These include requests to redirect grants earmarked for agricultural projects to building elementary schools, starting Catholic universities, or supporting youth conferences. Another example is to settle for lower building standards in order to get more houses for the same pool of funds. These are competing goods with noteworthy merits. But the possibility of CRS homes crumbling and crushing people at the next earthquake is unacceptable. Sometimes holding back monetary grants until overdue evaluations are received causes frustrations and accusations of lack of trust.

The principle of saving face applies to these difficult situations also. When noes are to be delivered, thought has to be given to the best way to do so and the best person to communicate the message. One can offer constructive pointers to increase the likelihood for future collaboration.

Because the noes are painful and not always avoidable, I have learned that it is prudent to approach relationships as a long game: look for opportunities to convey the yeses and to view these as good "investments." We should welcome requests that we can grant, not begrudge them. It is important to reach out to create positive rapport, particularly after a disappointing resolution. These prevent a sour note from hanging in the air for too long, and build up the social capital for navigating the ups and downs of relationships.

Navigating Cultural Hot Spots

Currently there is much debate and disagreement with the application of church teachings on major social and cultural issues to concrete decisions in ministries. These issues include sexual orientation, gay people in civil marriage, gender identity, use of contraceptives, and policies that directly or indirectly enable abortions.

The task is not simply applying canon law or doctrine to cut-and-dried situations governed by well-established and unified guidance. It is a process that constantly evolves, requiring attentiveness to developments in the social, civil, and legal arenas, and holding people and their well being at the center of our deliberations. This process is also spiritual in nature, calling for deep discernment, reliance on the Holy Spirit, and humility to accept that none of us alone has the whole truth.

It is the responsibility of leaders of Catholic ministries to maintain communion with the diocesan bishop. Bishops, as successors of the apostles, are ordained to continue the work of Christ. They do so through teaching, sanctifying, and governing. Under the bishops' direction, all apostolates are to seek close coordination and connection with the presbyterate. As the Second Vatican Council stated in its 1965 *Decree on the Bishops' Pastoral Office in the Church* (*Christus Dominus*), "Thus all undertakings and organizations, be they catechetical, missionary, charitable, social, familial, educational, or anything else pursuing a pastoral aim, should be directed toward harmonious action. Thus at the same time the unity of the diocese will also be made more evident" (no. 17).

With respect to the bishops' teaching, the same document instructs:

> The bishops should present Christian doctrine in a manner adapted to the needs of the times, that is to say, in a manner that will respond to the difficulties and questions by which people are especially burdened and troubled. They should also guard that doctrine, teaching the faithful to defend and propagate it. . . . Since it is the mission of the Church to converse with the human society in which it lives, it is especially the duty of bishops to seek out men and both request and promote dialogue with them. These conversations on salvation ought to be noted for clarity of speech as well as humility and mildness in order that at all times truth may be joined to charity and understanding with love. Likewise they should be noted for due prudence joined with trust, which fosters friendship and thus is capable of bringing about a union of minds. (no. 13)

That the Catholic Church does not permit gay marriage is clear. At the same time, the church also upholds the dignity of all individuals, recognizing that each one of us is made in the image of God. This gospel truth includes LGBTQ individuals who are, without exception, to be treated with care and compassion.

Bringing the two together in the context of organizations is not simple or always successful. Compounding the difficulty is that the issue of sexual orientation and identity cuts across a broad swath of organizational life, including, among other tasks, hiring, firing, and retention of LGBTQ personnel; selection of speakers or board members; what is "permitted" in the social media postings of colleagues; support of children from same-sex families in schools; permission to host LGBTQ student clubs and use of facilities for their functions; selection of hymns in parishes; and restrictions on display of gay support symbols or messages.

The handling of these situations can cause immense pain, disunity, and savage public attacks. Each one of these decisions is complex because it comes up against consideration of legislation, fair treatment of employees, or rights of expression. The intense focus can foster a dismembered view of people ignoring their totality and telescoping only on the one dimension in question. The focus is not just on the person, but also on the people who refuse to point fingers at the individual. People in these situations may lose their humanity as they become "problems" to be solved.

The divisive, harsh, and incendiary rhetoric that is tolerated and possibly encouraged is a tactic of war, not a manifestation of grace. It robs us of the opportunity to speak a gospel of love and to teach by example how we work through differences. No matter how passionate or correct we think we are, such differences can serve as invitations to subjugate our own agenda to the command of God to stay as one in Christ.

For CRS, one area that requires continuous vigilance is partnerships with organizations that do not engage in abortion services but support and distribute modern contraceptives. CRS's mission is to serve the poorest and most vulnerable across the world. The breadth and scope require extensive collaboration with other organizations that have established presence in communities that we cannot practically reach. Many areas in developing countries are geographically remote without good roads and transportation infrastructure. Sometimes we just do not have means to reach these communities.

Collaboration with these organizations involves the sharing of funds and expertise for which CRS has been criticized. Participation in professional associations, panels, and training programs to gain and share expertise in our areas of work has been seen as compromising our defense of church teachings. Yet these are exactly the forums and audiences for the church to communicate the efficacy of natural-family-planning methods and the reasons for our advocacy.

Some critics have suggested that CRS refrain from accepting funds from the US government given its positions on abortion, contraception, and same-sex marriage. Yet Catholics pay taxes, and the church engages the government in advocacy for various policies, lobbies for vouchers to support Catholic education, and fights for funding to offer Catholic healthcare and social services to the poor.

The church, by Christ's command, chooses to go out into the world and does not cut itself off from the world. It thereby accepts the challenge to evangelize in a pluralistic, polarized, and secular society. As such, the intersection of church teaching and organizational practices will continue to present challenges. The application, for example, of DEI (diversity, equity, and inclusiveness) in church ministries will present seeming contradictions.

My experience at CRS points to the necessity of working closely with the church hierarchy. Accepting and anticipating these difficulties, CRS instituted a standing committee comprising theologians and bishops to formulate frameworks and guidelines to define the space for appropriate actions and partnerships. Our field leaders establish relationships with the local bishops through periodic meetings, briefings, and alerts to upcoming issues. The bishop board chairs I worked with have approached the problems as partners, teachers, and elders who hold the good of our team, our beneficiaries, and the church simultaneously in their hearts.

Over several decades of working with church ministries, I have been in and seen situations whereby doctrine eclipsed and bypassed other considerations. Communications then became assertions of authority rather than the search for common purpose. Even then, restraint, grace, and forgiveness have sometimes prevented irreversible ruptures of relationships and maintained sufficient goodwill for a future day.

Unity calls us to hold these difficulties in prayer and in genuine consultation, with presumption of one another's goodness and fidelity. We need to enable processes to evolve through dialogue and learning. Our generosity is the willingness to manage differences at the level of interpretation, application, and approaches without losing sight that we are one body of Christ.

As different surfaces of a prism reflect light differently, we bring gifts to help one another address the signs of the time without being fearful. We must hold the faces of people affected by these decisions in our deliberations. When vexed, frustrated, or at an impasse, we reach for space for prayerful discernment. Joined in ministry and evangelization, we are not competitors bent on winning, getting our way, or gaining the upper hand based on differential power and resource positions. There is no winning except to serve better and to bear witness to God's presence here and now.

The light that we reflect is the light of Christ. It is ever new, ever revealing. To both act in and bring forth this light, we must remain open to new insight, cultivate the humility to remember that we do not have the whole truth, and let the Holy Spirit work in us.

Challenges and conflicts can be the grist for holiness. Leaders make that choice and act accordingly.

4

Reflection on
"Feminine Genius"

To counter the perception that women are of no value to the church, multiple papal documents have lifted up women, particularly highlighting their feminine genius. These descriptions are presented in Chapter 2.

While well intentioned, these references are packed with platitudes and stereotypes. Almost saintly measures of patience, endurance, sensitivity, and gentleness are attributed to women. The "feminine" qualities are commendable, but they are definitely neither universal of all women nor unique only to women. Women are not beyond the realm of human flaws and foibles.

While women are bathed in the glow of the Blessed Mother through their motherhood, men, fathers, husbands, brothers, and male caretakers need not be precluded from the above depictions. In my family, my husband is definitely the one with greater patience; he is the work-at-home dad on the frontline of applying bandaids, soothing disappointments, cautioning unkind judgments, and leading our sons in volunteer service at the homeless center.

Pope Francis has himself been described as the best model of the Blessed Mother: "Pope Francis is a shining example of feminine genius: patient, tender, showing mercy and love."[1] In raising up women, we should be careful not to stereotype men in a way that diminishes their wholeness or makes caricatures of them, in the same manner as has been done to women.

Stereotypes are also unhelpful for the promotion of women. The popular attributions to women derive from longstanding gender roles for the external work–internal care division of labor. These roles have been changing dramatically as women and men, out of necessity or preference, increasingly assume economic, parenting, and home responsibilities that blur and cross gender lines.

Unchecked, we may reinforce a rigidity delineating "women's jobs" versus "men's jobs." Such classification, often implicit, has stood in the way of opening up opportunities for women. Across different sectors, barriers crumble when women are elected as student body presidents or senators; appointed CEOs, judges, and generals; and recruited as surgeons, astronauts, scientists, journalists, and sportscasters. The gain is not just the shattering of glass ceilings for senior positions. It is also the demolition of the "he can / she cannot" bias that has kept women out. For the church, outside of positions that require the jurisdiction of ordained clergy, opportunities for women in leadership can be opened up, as Pope Francis has done, by rethinking traditional "men's jobs."

We must also be cautious in casting women as agreeable, pliant, pleasant, or tender. Many times women have to be "difficult" to challenge prevailing practices; "audacious" to speak truth to power; "high maintenance" to insist on action; "critical" to point out what is not working; "pushy" to overcome inertia; "competitive" to prove legitimacy; or "ambitious" to want to do more and be more.

---

[1] Ulla Gumundson, quoted in Josh J. McElwee, "Vatican Event Tackles Women's Equality, Inclusion, Ordination," *National Catholic Reporter*, March 9, 2015.

We do not want the absence of these qualities to be the selling points for women. That would be taming women, not empowering them. By other lenses these behaviors would be praised as courage, strength, tenacity, honesty, grit, and commitment. When assessing women, we should be watchful and avoid implicitly internalizing standards set by crusty cultural conventions.

In *A Living Gospel,* Robert Ellsberg makes the same point in his discussion of how women saints often have been portrayed:

> Traditional accounts of women saints—almost always written by men—have tended to emphasize "feminine virtues: of purity, humble service, obedience, or patient endurance. . . . Needless to say, such labels elide the range of functions such women may have performed, whether as theologians, prophets, healers, visionaries, or trailblazers in spiritual life. The process of canonization often excels in conforming saints to a stereotypical mold. The first thing we ought to do is break through these molds and to see instead how holy women also questioned authority, defied restrictive codes and models of behavior, and displayed audacity and wit in surmounting the obstacles placed in their paths.[2]

The leadership capacities described in the prior chapter are not delineated along gender lines. These capacities are necessary for both men and women who lead faith-based ministries. Research has shown that the healthiest people develop both their feminine and masculine traits, leveraging analytical thinking with intuition and managing for accountability while exercising care for others.

---

[2] Robert Ellsberg, *A Living Gospel: Reading God's Story in Holy Lives* (Maryknoll, NY: Orbis Books, 2019), 128–29.

Support for women must allow for imperfection and the room for them to make their own mistakes and grow from them. It is not fair to judge women leaders by a standard of perfection, place them under the microscopes, and focus only on their missteps. Women are not always collaborative, sensitive, or generous. They too can be blinded by ambition, tempted by power, and stymied by self-doubt. What women leaders need for success is not hyped expectations, but the commitment of organizations to let them come into their own and grow into their full potential.

The heightened attention to women has led to the suggestion for a theology of women. Pope Francis remarked, "I think that we haven't yet come up with a profound theology of the woman in the Church."[3] This emanates from the perception that women are a mystery. It situates women as a species separate from men, or from the human family. Both women and men are holy mysteries; both bear the image of God.

The distinctions made about women remind me of a funny story in my own family. My brother is married to a Caucasian woman. When their firstborn, Matthew, was about two years old, my siblings wanted the toddler to have a sense of his Chinese heritage. Trekking through Chinatown in Toronto, we pointed out to him all things Chinese: Chinese food (dim sum), funny-smelling vegetables and herbs, birds kept in Chinese-style cages, and décor heavy on the theme of dragons and phoenixes. At the end of the excursion when asked what he learned from the day, Matthew replied, "I know I am half Chinese and half human."

As a student of organizations and practitioner for over forty years, instead of a theology of women, I would propose sociological, organizational, and ethical assessments to inform the recruitment and development of women leaders. These consultations unveil the biases and practices that have kept women at

---

[3] Quoted in Emily Reimer-Barry, "Constructing a New Theology of Women," *US Catholic*, January 21, 2015.

a "safe" distance. The results form the groundwork to change practices and attitudes.

Where there are differences in behavior between men and women, I find the cause to be different experiences rather than different natures. In many countries the care of the family falls completely on women. Women make life work for spouses, children, parents, in-laws, even neighbors. They face myriad demands to which they respond without formal power or sufficient financial resources. They are the first responders when something goes wrong. Women attend to the needs of this day, get ready for tomorrow, and cast an eye to what their families need for the future.

Women's reality is bracketed by dependence and interdependence. They absorb and endure the full brunt of decisions made by their husbands and other authority figures. Out of necessity and culture, women rely on one another almost by instinct: listening, accommodating, seeking common interests, cooperating, and doing their part for the whole to function. With few resources, they do not act in the theoretical or hypothetical realms, but with unyielding pragmatism.

Women learn to bargain with lenders for loan extensions; they walk miles to bring a child to the clinic; they save and buy a few chickens or goats to generate tuition for their children; they barter to get needed services. Women are the first to give up eating when food becomes scarce. Sometimes they give away or sell their children when they are at the end of their rope. In humanitarian work, empowering women is regarded as the best investment to reduce malnutrition, poverty, and child abuse. Resources given to women increase the well being and education levels of children, prevent trafficking, and shorten the duration of violent conflicts.

When these women are given the chance to speak, it is seldom from personal ego, but from the urgency that their families and communities depend on them to make the case. This is true too of women religious and nonprofits that serve them. Their frame of reference is not doctrine or judgment, but the paths to enable human well being and flourishing.

The inclusion of women as participants and leaders is important to the church not so much because of the innate virtues implied by the assignation of feminine genius, but because women bring experiences different from those of men, particularly those of ordained clergy. Their daily experiences cultivate perspectives, skills, approaches, and priorities that tend not to be part of the lived experience of male leaders. Women, when respectfully engaged, will raise problems and solutions that educate and expand the imagination of decision makers. As Pope Francis observed, women are more practical in their thinking and more decisive on their recommendations.

It is important for women to be included in decision making and not have other people chosen to represent their interests. We have learned from different social movements that it is neither empowering nor optimal for those in power to serve as the "voice for the voiceless." The "voiceless," when formally included, can speak for themselves about their challenges, priorities, and preferences. They should not rely on the patronage and goodwill of others to make their case. Nothing short of formalized representation confers the gravitas, rights for self-determination, and acceptance accorded to insiders.

One woman leader, Kerry Robinson, writes:

> For those who value the church's mission and vitality, its impact as a global humanitarian network and the restoration of trust in church leadership, concern about the role of women is a matter of managerial and moral urgency.
>
> How compromised is the church by failing to include women at the highest levels of leadership and at the tables

of decision-making in the Roman Curia and throughout the institutional church? Nearly every institution in the world has accommodated and incorporated women in leadership—often reluctantly at first—only to admit the practical, tangible value of having done so. Corporations with women on their boards have a better return for shareholders; woman doctors are less likely to be sued for malpractice; universities, the military, the judiciary, government—are all strengthened by the presence of women in leadership and decision-making. . . . To be clear, it is not that women are smarter, more judicious or holier than men. Each of us is inherently myopic on our own or within our own uniform groups. We only know what we know. We need and benefit from a diversity of perspectives and experiences to be wiser and more prudent.[4]

Implicit to the inclusion of women as leaders is the issue of power. Many people are not comfortable with the mention of power. Some women leaders downplay their position of power and authority. They are more comfortable citing other sources of power such as expertise, relationships, or dedication. At the same time, we recognize the injustice when women are excluded from formal authority and leadership positions. Through the ages they have been left to navigate through personal influence, cajoling, seeking favors, or bending the ear of someone else to represent their viewpoints. These informal sources of power are important, but they should not preclude formal recognition of women's capacity to lead. Formal power is akin to having a vote that will be counted. From inclusion and institutional authorization, women are no longer "guests" whose good manners and pleasant repartee make it more likely they will procure a return invitation.

---

[4] Kerry Alys Robinson, "Women Must Be at Tables Where Church Decisions Are Made," *Chicago Catholic*, September 4, 2019.

Power can be abusive. It can lead to exploitation, inappropriate use of rewards, and the brandishing of "big sticks." Women and men both have to be self-aware of such misuse. But good can come from organizational power that is given as a currency to guide the entity toward its mission. It confers legitimacy to provide direction, and the spotlight to set the tone for expected behavior. Power is like fire: used rightly, it builds civilization; used wrongly, it destroys. The call here is not to strive for power. The point is that women are not by nature less equipped to handle power or less worthy to be entrusted with its use.

While many worry about misuse, the greater concern for me is the underuse of power. Frequently I hear the frustration of people about leaders when they fail to lead. Such leaders can leave an organization to meander, improvements and innovations to go unexplored, and significant inefficiencies to diminish productivity. When leaders do not call for accountability, toxic behavior can go unchecked.

When I was in my thirties, I was elected chair of my professional division at the Academy of Management. I had little experience as an elected officer and became absorbed with running meetings well. My major goal was to master Robert's Rules of Order, a protocol I had not learned in my Hong Kong days. I studied past meeting agendas and notes and became conversant with motions, discussions, and approvals. I completed my term with flying colors, I believed, because there were no missteps in the way I chaired meetings.

The chair who succeeded me started his first meeting with a list of improvements he thought we should consider. These included ways to support junior faculty coming into the field: create a separate award for them so that they do not have to compete head on with researchers with decades more experience, offer workshops and mentoring opportunities, and introduce them to journal editors and other gatekeepers who can have a big impact on their success.

I realized then I had done nothing in my leadership year. I did not use my position and the privilege of agenda setting and convening to serve our members. I was so absorbed with form that I forgot about substance. It was the best lesson I learned, as it revealed to me why people endow and charge others with formal power. It is to look after the organization.

In closing, let me quote from Professor Catherine Hilkert in a personal note to me:

> Yet all power is the gift of the Holy Spirit and is meant to be exercised for the building up of the body of Christ and for the church's witness in and for the world. The question should not be a matter of anyone seeking "officialdom" or "prestige" or "power over." Rather, there are women gifted with various forms of leadership within and for the body of Christ, and the church's witness and way of operating would be more authentic if we were to recognize and call forth that leadership.[5]

The inclusion of women is simply the principle of subsidiarity at work and imitation of Jesus's hospitality to women as friends and disciples in mission.

---

[5] Correspondence with Sr. Mary Catherine Hilkert, professor of theology, University of Notre Dame, Notre Dame, Indiana, February 19, 2016.

5

Acting
for Women's Leadership

This chapter focuses on what we can do to make women's leadership a more frequent reality. How do we move into a future where the recruitment of women becomes part of an established routine? What practices create a work environment that fosters the development of women and that enables them to thrive? Note that men also flourish in environments that are attentive to women's needs.

The autobiographical essays in the book show that some paths to leadership in Catholic ministries follow linear professional progressions, while some do not. Those that do include Sr. Carol's progression from nurse to administrator, president of a Catholic hospital, and then leadership of the Catholic Health Association. Similarly, Laura Kaiser rose through a series of positions in hospitals to become the chief of the SSM hospital system. In Catholic education teachers and faculty like Cyril Cruz and Julie Sullivan demonstrated their interest and talent for administration, rising through the ranks to their respective positions as principal and university president. Annemarie Reilly and Kerry Weber started their careers in the organizations that they eventually rose to lead.

Other journeys took unexpected turns. Sr. Donna, an organizational psychologist, went from leading a mental health ministry to presiding over Catholic Charities USA. From civil service and volunteer work for the church, Ana Phares was spotted to fill the vacancy for the presidency of the local Catholic Charities. Ann Manion was an accountant and volunteer girls' soccer coach before she founded the Women's Care Center. Having no expertise in international humanitarian relief, I left my life as an academic administrator to lead Catholic Relief Services. The commonality of these paths is probably the whisper of the Holy Spirit.

Therefore the recruitment and development of women for Catholic ministries and eventually for leadership must work at different levels from different vantage points. I look at three here: (1) Catholic ministries that employ women, (2) outside organizations that offer leadership training, and (3) planting the seed for women's leadership in girls and young adults.

Church Ministries

Catholic ministries clearly play a large role in the recruitment, development, and advancement of women. Recruitment must commit to active identification of women candidates before a search can be considered complete. Pope Francis noted that any position available to a lay man should also be made available to a lay woman. These include not only staff positions, but membership on councils, boards, and advisory committees.

Not infrequently good intentions seem to be stymied by a lack of candidates. For example, a large Catholic health system had difficulty finding women candidates to serve on the boards of its local hospitals. It had retained an international executive search firm to identify multiple candidates for future appointments. The search firm reached out to me asking for names and described how difficult this assignment was. It just did not know where to start.

When it reached out for ideas, I pointed out how all Catholic universities issue publications that routinely feature their alumnae. The content includes awards by the university, announcement of appointments and promotions, special interest stories, and so on. Each university releases two to four such publications a year. Proper collection and logging of this information across all Catholic universities would provide a treasure trove of names.

These and other Catholic periodicals often report on speakers, seminars, and conferences, another source of names. In addition, parents and alumni of local Catholic schools are good sources for local candidates. Tapping into Catholic national associations of universities, K-12 schools, health ministries, campus ministries, social services, communication agencies, chief administrators, and more can yield fruitful results. I am admittedly judgmental, but the notion that talented Catholic women are hard to find reflects that we have not yet looked *seriously*. They are not rare.

Catholic organizations in which women currently work present opportunities for developing and advancing women. As positions open, it is important to list the qualifications needed explicitly and establish a clear process for application and evaluation. Commit to interviewing internal candidates and involve colleagues in the interview and assessment process. These practices prevent the perception that people with authority bring in their friends, or that people from the inside are not good enough.

When possible, presentations by candidates should be open to all. Colleagues learn from watching candidates; they may see strengths they want to develop; they get a feel for what is expected of candidates from the opposite side of the table. At the same time, colleagues see the aspiration and values of the ministry as reflected in the candidates who are finally hired.

Beyond recruitment, other policies play critical roles in fostering an environment in which women and other employees can flourish. Flexibility in work schedules and locations, as we have seen in the response to the pandemic, has a profound contribution to the work-life balance of staff. They are actually more productive and committed. Allowing the transfer of unused vacation and sick days to colleagues promotes a sense of community. Matching contributions to pension plans encourages saving and offers a safety net.

I do realize that Catholic ministries are often strapped for money, but pay and benefits to staff hold moral and practical consequences that should not be taken lightly. Ministries should expend energy to understand what staff members really prioritize (such as flexibility to attend to personal and familial needs, good healthcare provision, savings support) and shop for the most efficient package aligned with their priorities.

Commitment to pay equity is a moral obligation. The process begins with a hard look at the pay differences between men and women in comparable jobs, with similar skills, tenure, and performance histories. Having factored in the above, are there inequalities? Are these exceptions, or do they reflect a systemic bias? What is the strategy for closing these gaps? Over what period of time?

Organizational culture has significant influence on work satisfaction. It can be enhanced through "360 reviews"—feedback from not only a manager but peers—so that people at all levels of the organization get feedback on their strengths, gaps, and effect on others. Such surveys offer an honest look in terms of whether colleagues feel respected for their views, supported in their work, and primed for future opportunities. Common now are "pulse surveys"—short spurts of questions—to get real-time responses and ideas. Open, regular, and interactive communication up and down the organization fosters understanding, transparency, and buy-in.

Women in church ministries, like peers in other sectors, yearn for professional development and continuing education. These allow them to learn new skills, broaden their perspectives, and enlarge their vision. Again, lack of resources seems to put the development of staff on the back burner. Yet money is really not the primary enabler.

There are extensive online programs that are affordable, and sometimes courses from universities are made available to nonprofits for free. In recent years I have been trying to learn about climate change and the energy transition on my own. Numerous reports and papers are posted online. Not a week goes by without notices for forums, reports, discussion, and so on. Registration for these is free.

A greater obstacle than money is the absence of a strong focus on learning and development in many organizations. Learning can be instituted and supported through monthly gatherings for presentations on specific books, reports, or deep dives on high-performing peers. Meetings can routinely incorporate a succinct set of points from professional meetings that staff attended. Personnel reviews should include discussions of a colleague's desired areas for growth, and the learning agenda to achieve these. Specific numbers of work hours can be allocated toward learning activities with completion of these noted in performance reports. Explicit expectations and support, rather than money, set learning and development in motion.

Female staff also speak wistfully about their desire for mentoring. There just isn't much, particularly in parish ministries. Research has shown that people tend to do better in organizations when they have access to coaching (from a supervisor or an experienced peer), mentoring (from a higher-level colleague who takes an interest in the progression of the staff member), and sponsorship (from a member of the executive team who actively promotes the individual for advancement).

Human flourishing tends to come from people who take an interest in us, recognize our potential, and help us get there. They help us see the bigger pictures, put challenges into perspectives, and offer constructive feedback. Although both men and women benefit from these investments, research indicates that these are particularly important to the advancement of women in organizations.

As clericalism has been cited by the holy fathers as an obstacle to empowering women in the church, we hope seminary education will take up this issue. It should (1) call attention to the role of women in Christ's ministry, their contribution to evangelization and faith formation, and their examples of missionary discipleship; (2) address the mandate for co-responsibility, what it entails, and how to move from promise to reality; (3) provide opportunities during the years of formation for seminarians to work with and for women; and (4) hold a mirror to the bias against women.

Women's Development Resources

Recent years have witnessed an explosion of conferences, councils, and facilitated conversations to highlight the contributions of women to the church. These seek to listen to women's critiques, solicit their ideas, and cultivate their capacity for leadership roles.

Since 2014, Voices of Faith has assembled Catholic women from around the world annually at the Vatican on International Women's Day. These women meet with cardinals and various leaders from the Curia to share their vision, challenges, and the precarious conditions for women in many parts of the world. They recount stories of service and sacrifice in the pursuit of social and economic justice. The purpose of Voices of Faith, according to its website, is to "empower and advocate for a prophetic Catholic Church where women's voices count, participate, and lead on an equal footing with men."

Women of the Church, a conference hosted by the Sisters of St. Benedict of Ferdinand, Indiana, partnered with Saint Meinrad

Seminary and School of Theology, convened its first and fully subscribed gathering in 2016. Buoyed by this success the conference held its second event in 2019. Also in 2016 the Council of Major Superiors created GIVEN, a leadership conference that recruited three hundred women, mostly in their twenties, for a week of gathering. This leadership event was repeated in 2019 and 2021. Across the land women's assemblies, dialogues, and councils are being hosted by multiple dioceses including San Diego, Philadelphia, Arlington, Toledo, Sioux Falls, and others.

In addition to the gatherings, resources have also been invested for the development of women's skills and readiness for leadership. The National Council of Catholic Women has established "Leadership, Training, and Development (LTD): A Council Enrichment Program," which offers one-day or two-day training programs customized for the needs of the members. Its website lists fifty topic areas including change management, effective committees, volunteer management, job descriptions, action plans, mentoring, and more.

The Leadership Collaborative, offered by the Leadership Council of Women Religious (LCWR), offers programs to enhance the capacity for transformational leadership among women's religious orders, their associates, and their partners. The Leadership Collaborative website (thelc.global) states:

> The Collaborative Leadership Development Programs (CLDP) are programs sponsored by the Leadership Collaborative. It is an 18-month integrative process with an intercultural perspective, designed to prepare participants with the skills, knowledge and confidence to assume leadership positions in community and ministry. The CLDP blends contemplative practices and building relationships with self-growth and spiritual development, through prayerful study and interaction, online forums, mentoring, and coaching.

What we need at this point is a central location to post the information relating to women's leadership for church ministries. Currently information on conferences, development programs, papers, reports, tools, videos, networks, and upcoming events is scattered. Such a website could also post openings for paid positions, board positions, advisory committees, and so on. Learning hubs could be self-organized by members on different topics and queries for benchmarking or peer learning.

Planting the Seed Early

It is possible but not likely that a young woman would wake up one morning and declare her vocation to serve the church. In the essays of our women leaders there was long gestation with some beginning in very early childhood. Berni Neal felt the love of the Blessed Mother and St. Bernadette when she watched the movie *The Song of Bernadette.* Kerry Weber's journey to Catholic journalist and executive editor began with visits to the diocesan newspaper where her mother worked.

These are unique examples, but they do illustrate how a journey begins: through exposure, impressions, small actions, discernment, and eventually commitment. For women to serve as professionals in the church, they must have a sense that there are meaningful roles for them. They need to believe that their gifts will be valued and they will be welcomed.

They come to these conclusions with the stories they hear from parents, grandparents, godparents, and whoever read to them to feed their imagination. There are many stories written of inspiring and courageous women of faith. By their faith, efforts, and boldness, Catholic women through the ages have contributed to the doctrine, intellectual tradition, and service outreach of the church. They have been at the frontier of health and educational apostolates: creating, growing, and innovating to meet the needs of the people who came to them.

If we do not see women portrayed visibly in the mass readings, they are in the context: Rebecca, Hannah, Deborah, Ruth, Mary Magdalene, Mary of Bethany, Martha, and the disciples Priscilla, Dorcas, and Phoebe, who formed part of the human chain that enabled St. Paul's ministry. Walk by any Catholic school, university, or hospital and probe its beginning, and you are likely to find heroic nuns who leaned on the Holy Spirit and willed the ministry into being. Today, contemporary women of faith continue the work to support life, fight injustice, serve the marginalized, form young people, and stand with prisoners.

It becomes our task to know and recount the faith and contribution of these women, to make these stories come to life to feed the imagination and fire the inspiration of our children. These histories need to become a part of formal studies, whether in CCD instruction or as part of the curricula of Catholic schools. Formal instruction raises the gravitas of the subject matter beyond cultural lore to a systematic part of our past where women as well as men responded faithfully and courageously to help bring about God's kingdom.

Two things need to happen to make the leadership of women real for girls and young women: (1) they need to see it in action, and (2) at some point they need to become part of the action. It is much easier to conclude that women can provide leadership in the church when they have seen a woman director of youth ministries giving direction and breathing spirit into the programs; a female parish council member giving the financial report to the parish; priests consulting with or deferring to women co-pastors; a female superintendent excitedly sharing her goals for K–12, and their mothers making the case to initiate a program never tried before.

The engagement of young people, particularly girls in their teen years, gives them a sense of the work of the church and their role in it. They become part of the adult community, assuming responsibility for making God real in their communities. Oftentimes they are recruited as volunteer labor: painting fences, cleaning up playgrounds, teaching lessons, or packing food. Recruit them instead for volunteer leadership. Make available training in problem solving, team building, and design thinking, and give them license to innovate and add their own touches. Use these engagements as access points for observing and understanding the systemic and social roots of problems, and implications for them as Christians. Through this process, both faithfulness and leadership unfold.

Reasons for Kerry Robinson's call that "women must be at tables where church decisions are made in the church" are well established and advocated at the highest level of the church.[1] But it is not yet the church's natural instinct. There are obstacles, but these are no match for what we can do.

Ultimately, this call is not for women. It is for the vitality of the church as one body in Christ to love as Christ loves. Would the Holy Spirit settle for anything less?

---

[1] Kerry Alys Robinson, "Women Must Be at Tables Where Church Decisions Are Made," *Chicago Catholic*, September 4, 2019.

PART II

REQUISITE CAPACITIES FOR LEADERSHIP

In this Part I offer four capacities that I consider essential for those exercising leadership in Catholic ministries. Based on decades of teaching, practice, and observing leadership, I have classified the requisite attributes, behaviors, and skills into four types of capacities: capacity for others; capacity for self-reflection and growth; capacity for alignment; and capacity for Christian witness.

The first three capacities are applicable to all organizations: faith-based or secular, corporate or not-for-profit. The last capacity, that for Christian witness, is unique to faith-based ministries. While Chapter 2 described a set of attributes demonstrated by the women leaders contributing to this book, this part of the book recommends a set of capacities for consideration by all leaders, men and women alike.

Leadership, particularly at the very top of the pyramid, assumes full responsibility for the outcome of the entire enterprise. As the saying goes, "The buck stops here." Without downloading the litany in a management textbook, full responsibility encompasses direction setting, effective implementation through formal structure and systems, and constructive engagements with internal and external stakeholders. Leaders are also stewards of a culture that defines the shared beliefs, norms, and boundaries of the organization.

Many things need to be done well: good listening, good communication, ability to motivate colleagues, understanding external trends and their implications, setting standards and holding people accountable, driving innovation and change in management. At the same time leaders need to be resolute but flexible, politically astute and ethical, and compassionate while insisting on accountability. Instead of an ad hoc list of "to do's," I offer four types of capacities to organize our thinking.

6

Capacity for the Other

The women leaders in this book all hail the importance of treating their colleagues with respect and attention. They call for careful listening and openness to other people's ideas. They note the importance of an authentic appreciation and recognition of the contributions and gifts of others. These women do not attribute success to themselves but to their teams. Most important, these leaders find great satisfaction in helping others grow and mentoring other women to succeed.

Let me share an anecdote of which I am not proud but from which I learned a lot. At one point in my career, hosting multiple formal dinners a week was routine. I became slightly resentful of the claim on my evenings and grew weary with small talk. To make the time spent on dinner more productive and fun, I would call ahead and ask to be seated with specific colleagues to get caught up. Now, knowing the rationale and efforts behind table assignments, I probably caused headaches. After a few times, guilt set in and I decided to stop this practice.

I realized that I was only thinking about myself, not my own responsibility to be a good host. While the dinner may be the third in five days for me, such dinners for the guests may be a once-a-year or once-in-a-lifetime event. I had been shirking my duty. But what mortified me more was that I did not try to get to know these people, to understand the life journeys that took them to that banquet. How come I had no curiosity about them? Why did I see them as a duty, not as persons who had a special claim to be there? Why did I allow small talk, a warm-up essential, to become the full course?

At my master's graduation a long time ago, a speaker whose name I can no longer recall spoke a message I could not forget. He raised the term *charisma* and asked what that is about. Immediately the audience shouted examples ranging from Hitler to Jesus. He said: "Charisma is the ability to take people as you find them, to like them for who they are, and to not despise them for what they are not. This is as old as the gospel and as new as *Godspell*." The latter reference provides the carbon dating of the century and decade for my master's graduation ceremony!

I took this advice to heart and with new resolve applied this to the dinner guests I was assigned to host. I operated on the principle that all people come with interesting stories. Human dramas are spun from life's highs and lows, the priorities that guide choices, and the dreams that keep people going. In these, holiness finds its home.

I would start with safe and fun topics to highlight the reasons for their presence that evening. Questions such as: What is your relationship to this institution? Why this cause? How did you meet your spouse? How many children? Grandchildren? Was your career pretty much a straight path? Or were there bends and reversals? What is the most important quality you want your children to have? I never ran out of questions.

I took in not just the content of the answers but the joy and gratitude that tumbled forth. In a way our conversations were prayers. The words held the compositions of life, and for many, the blessings of God in light and dark moments.

On a humorous note, my table companions would tell me that I am really smart. Yet, I did not speak a word of intellectual heft.

All I did was ask them about themselves, enter into the drama of their lives, and celebrate with them in genuine appreciation. Paraphrasing that long-ago speaker: Charisma is the ability to draw other people to yourself. It turns out that the focus on them, the ability to like them for who they are, and the invitation for them to share what means the most to them is the glue that binds us. This dynamic also proves the adage that people may not remember what you tell them, but they remember how you make them feel. If I ever have a chance for another career, I would interview people and approach these interviews as prayer. In the meantime, I do not really need a formal studio; this could be how I approach people.

The leadership literature and the women leaders in this book all speak to the importance of empathy and compassion. Empathy is the ability to put ourselves in another person's shoes and to allow ourselves to feel the plight of others. Compassion involves action to relieve their suffering. It could be as simple as reducing work demands, organizing fund and food drives, donating, volunteering, and so forth. There is a massive literature developing on the discovery of "mirror neurons" that link empathy and compassion to their biological building blocks.

While empathy and compassion compose the language of human relations, leadership, particularly in ministry settings, requires more. Leadership of others must avoid using others only for our own interests or objectifying them as means to our own progress. Good leaders must commit to the people who work under their leadership. They must desire their employees' success and actively work for it. It starts with explicit efforts to identify the areas of strengths and needed growth of team members, matching these attributes to job responsibilities as much as possible. Leaders can facilitate professional growth through constructive feedback about what works and what needs improving. They follow up with resources to enable learning. When an employee is ready, leaders need to create stretch opportunities and coach the person through new challenges and lack of experience.

The genuine desire for other people's success is not a skill that one can pick up from a workshop. It requires an opening of the heart that truly rallies for the good of others. The capacity for others is an ongoing process of locating oneself between two necessary goods: the care of ourselves, and the care for others. A popular quotation from Rabbi Hillel sums this up: "If I am not for myself, who will be for me? If I am only for myself, what am I? And if not now, when?"

The above calls for a balance of "I" and "they." It eschews a self-centeredness that stems from a profoundly competitive system. We are rated and ranked since childhood; class assignments are based on different degrees of giftedness; we do not just engage in extracurricular activities but aim for leadership positions in them. Sports is a performance arena with its own metrics of playing times and statistics. While the win-loss column is only published in the newspaper under the sports section, it permeates the way we look at our lives. We keep score on ourselves and others.

Are other people competitors? Rivals? Is their gain our loss? Is our society by and large a zero-sum game? Unfortunately, when we look around, the deep inequality in our societies seems to bear this out. People with advantage claim the biggest pots while others have no paths to privilege. Even for those who do not subscribe to the "win at all costs" school of prospering, insecurities drive us to hold back and to look out only for ourselves.

The capacity for others begins with a deep assessment of these toxic views and behavior. The danger of these truisms is that they are self-fulfilling. When we subscribe to a "me first" logic and act on it, others respond accordingly. If this is the way we see the world and approach it, this becomes our world. We tumble into the company of "me first" people pulling one another down in a spiral of misery. As Rabbi Hillel's second question implies, when we fail to care for the other, we become a "what," no longer a "who."

For Christians, the gospel presents a countercultural view. Our world is not a zero-sum game; it is the expression of a loving God who wants us to flourish. Scarcity is not the blueprint, but abundance. If we are willing to look, we see the generosity of God mirrored in all the living things of creation, and particularly in the gift of one another. Scarcity is not the natural way, but the manufactured way when our appetites go awry, our fears grow unchecked, and our horizon turns inward.

From the very beginning God designed us as social beings who would find joy and love with and in one another. The Trinity is three Persons in one God, elating in continuous and unbounded love. By God's will we can flourish and find salvation only together, not singly, not on our own. Only as "we" can real progress and flourishing come to us. We cannot advance on the backs of one another, only hand in hand. Fraternity or social friendship lies at the center of our faith, a point made by Pope Francis in *Fratelli Tutti*.

The commandment to love our neighbors as ourselves is not to forego appropriate care of ourselves but to enable other people to enjoy this care. When we are ill, we do not refrain from going to a doctor in solidarity with those who have no doctors. Recognizing its benefit, we work to support universal access for those who have no healthcare. We do not send our children to nonperforming schools to stand with the poor but insist on resources for these schools to do a proper job.

At work, we want opportunities for growth, recognition, and promotion for ourselves. Good leaders also recognize these needs in the people they lead, and they commit to bringing others along. They shine the light on the contributions of their colleagues, leave the ladder down for their ascent, and add ramps for those who may need a different way up.

On a practical level, the capacity for others is not altruism; rather, it is a requisite for successful managing. It is the currency for trust. It is the magic that happens when people believe that their leaders really care for them. At daily mass in the Mendoza College of Business at the University of Notre Dame, Fr. Paul, our chaplain, would occasionally ask, "Carolyn, have you told these folks you love them lately?" I was usually too embarrassed to use this wonderful opening to tell my colleagues exactly that.

The capacity for other is also the currency for motivation. It has often been said that people do not care what you want from them until they know you care about them. Attending to colleagues makes for effective delegation because leaders do not simply give away the work they do not want. They invest in matching tasks with the staff person's skills, accomplishment to future promotability, and challenges to growth.

Successful collaboration with new partners both within and outside the organization is essential for the survival of organizations. This requires navigating through differences in perspectives and priorities. Such engagements have a better chance to succeed when there is willingness to work toward mutual benefits and not close the discussion until all parties gain. The capacity to understand people who disagree with us and acknowledge the legitimacy of their positions enables the search for common ground amid conflicts. Absence of this goodwill and the insistence on winning will drive parties apart and migrate toward polarization, where trench warfare takes over.

The mandate for DEI (diversity, equity, inclusiveness) is not just to add a couple more places at the table for the "other." It is the challenge to redefine "we," pushing outward the organization's boundary for the incorporation of the other into the whole. It requires us to be mindful of our own frame of reference and be humble when applying this as a yardstick on others. DEI cannot go far if we merely tolerate the differences of others. Until there is a genuine appreciation of and hunger for the gift of diversity in all realms of life—personal, biological, political—there will not be sufficient persistence to bring about genuine and lasting transformation. Otherwise DEI may find its resting place in the junkyard of well-intentioned programs that run out of steam.

Pope Francis has frequently encouraged a culture of encounter. It is the contrast to a culture of indifference whereby people's well being means nothing to us. An essay by Benjamin Durheim lists four elements of engagement he drew from theologian Karl Barth.[1] The first element is to see each other and behold the face that presents infinite qualities not reducible into categories or stereotypes. The second element is to listen and share, to disclose and take in, to know and be known in the exchange. The third element is to act: to not just be with the other but for the other. A spirit of gladness, the final element, enables all the other elements. Anything less, according to Barth, is mere accident and does not qualify as encounter.

Our engagement with the other emanates from God, who meets us in a spirit of gladness. We give of ourselves because we first receive from the bounty of God. In our care for the other, we mimic God; we return thanks; we bring God's grace to bear.

---

[1] Benjamin Durheim, "The Human as Encounter: Karl Barth's Theological Anthropology and a Barthian Vision of the Common Good," *Lumen et Vita* (June 2011): 1–20.

7

Capacity for Self-Awareness and Growth

Organizations have invested heavily in assessments to get a good read of their employees' strengths and weaknesses. For high-potential individuals in particular, a battery of questions is utilized to assess their readiness for leadership. One of the most important aspects is their degree of self-understanding and capacity for growth.

The primary concern is not the person's weakness. These are expected, because no person is perfect. Besides, different situations present different challenges, so that attributes that help a person succeed in one situation may be irrelevant or detrimental in other contexts. The primary purpose of evaluations is to point out adaptations that are necessary.

As individuals progress through their careers into a larger and more complex scope of responsibilities, the requisite strengths change. Early assignments call for managing oneself well, utilizing expertise in specific tasks, and delivering outputs that are timely, accurate, and reliable. The early environments are relatively bounded as demands and expectations tend to come from internal colleagues or a limited audience.

Leadership at the top of the organization calls for relying on others, managing across multiple boundaries, making decisions in situations of greater ambiguity, and tolerating greater risks and uncertainty. Leaders in these environments need to remain flexible while staying on course, pivot from one priority to another quickly, and relate to many stakeholders with different and sometimes contradictory demands. They must stay calm amid continuous disruptions and unexpected crises.

Leaders grow into these different skills through experience, experimentation, and trial and error. Effective evaluations point out strengths and gaps to provide the compass for course correction and development. An assessment inventory without gaps is one that has not looked deep enough into the individual.

The real test for leadership mettle comes in how individuals respond to these insights about them. Reactions reflect several key qualities: humility, care for one's impact on others, and adaptability. Humility acknowledges that one is not perfect, not always right, and may not have lived up to one's opinion of self. When humility is missing, feedback is cast as unfair, inaccurate, and undeserved. With such interpretation, feedback for improvement is taken as an affront and attack, not as the investment and commitment that it can become. Feedback can be taken as a friend or as a foe.

Quite often, feedback focuses on the impact of the individuals on their colleagues. Some leaders unlock potential in others, while others become obstacles and make work more difficult. A leader can push too hard or fail to give enough direction. Good intentions do not necessarily lead to good outcomes. A message given is not always the message received. Some leaders do not have a good sense of timing or tone for how questions are raised. Feedback enables people to look at themselves through the experiences of others. The capacity to make necessary adjustments reflects not only adaptability, but concern for others' well being and the quality of their work environment. Thus, self-awareness often becomes a table stake for aspiring leaders. This is particularly important for leaders given their power, prominence, and influence on team members' work environment, assignments, and sense of self-worth.

The ability to take feedback, improve, and change is linked to the concept of mindsets. Carol Dweck, a developmental psychologist, contrasts two mindsets.[1] People with fixed mindsets tend to tie learning to natural talents enabling them to be good in some things and not in others. There is only limited room for modification. In contrast, people who operate with growth mindsets tend to view skills, mastery, and new behavior as changeable and achievable through learning and experimentation. If the multiplication table does not come easily, we just have not found the right approach that connects the learner to the concept. Failures are just different steps in the discovery process giving us cues for the next steps.

Each of us adopts both mindsets regarding different aspects of our lives. I think of myself as a learner of new concepts, thus allowing me to broaden my knowledge sets to keep track of forty years of managerial challenges. In contrast, I do not think I have any athletic abilities and have been afraid to swim or ride a bike for the last fifty years. I am not artistic but am excited to take lessons to see if I could learn the basics of drawing.

For leaders, it is important to have growth mindsets for learning about their environments, acquiring relational skills, assessing their biases, and cultivating openness for new approaches. Research has shown that people who see themselves as capable of change and growth also hold the same positive belief about others. As such, growth-minded people are more willing to look at their prejudices, use different frames to understand old grievances, let go of past judgments, and undertake difficult steps toward the resolution of longstanding conflicts.

---

[1] Carol S. Dweck, "Mindsets of Human Nature: Promoting Change in the Middle-East, the Schoolyard, the Racial Divide, and Will Power," 2011 Award for Distinguished Scientific Contributions, *American Psychologist* (November 2012): 614–22.

We also need to know our own joys and fears. To break away from the competitive mindset, it is important to focus on what holds meaning and purpose for us. This is our compass, and it does not work well for guiding us on other people's journeys. It is untenable to deploy what society deems successful as the benchmark of our worth. When we calibrate ourselves by others' accomplishments, we find joy only when others are beneath us or have less than us. Even then, plagued by the thought of being overtaken, the joy of winning is fleeting. This attitude does not foster thanksgiving. It breeds self-pity and dishonors the source of all gifts.

In contrast, we need to know what gives us joy. It will lead us down the path that celebrates who we are and the work that only we can do for God. We are not more or less by what others achieve. We are not even more or less by our own efforts. We are what we are: winning does not add to that, and losing does not take away from it. While rankings, records, and first places can be lost, our gifts are part of us. They are ours to enjoy, build a life by, and offer to others. As a colleague told me once: Where we place in any competition is not a measure of our giftedness, but where those gifts can do the most good.

Many people get in their own way because they act out of their insecurities or their fear of being less. They are reluctant to share their gifts, credits, or opportunities. Insecurities fester in low self-esteem despite the magnificence other people can see in them. They do not see their gifts themselves, or regard them as transient.

Faced with the invitation to leave Notre Dame and join CRS, I could not make up my mind. I approached my spiritual director, Fr. Ken, and offered to share my analyses. His observation: If analyses were the key to the problem, I would not be seeking his counsel. His advice: Get in touch with my joys and fears.

Indeed, the fears woke me up midsleep. They involved giving up tenure, not knowing the basics of development work, and fear for my safety because CRS works in high-conflict areas. Different insights came, and the fears lost their grip on me.

My joy was simple. I came from women who lived through the Second World War. My mother was a war bride who gave birth to two children when she and my father were on the run from Japanese occupation. My aunt's schooling was terminated at fifth grade by the war. My beloved nanny became a servant girl at the age of nine to support her widowed mother and three younger siblings. The Maryknoll Sisters who educated me for twelve years exuded insuppressible spirit serving in mission. My joy in joining CRS: I was going home to people I may not have met but know intimately.

8

Capacity for Alignment

The position of the chief executive or equivalent confers the highest authority and assigns the ultimate responsibility for alignment. At my first meeting with CRS colleagues, I told them that while they are working very hard heads down, my job is to be heads up, to make sure that collectively we do not work ourselves into a blind alley. It is also my responsibility to see to it that our organizational arrangements provide a healthy and energizing environment to support and leverage their work. These are the outcomes of proper alignment.

A most unlikely source of inspiration for understanding alignment came to me from babies.

As I returned to work after my maternity leave for the birth of my older son, colleagues teased, "What does strategic management [my area of focus] mean when caring for a baby?" My response was that I was totally at the baby's beck and call, doing whatever the baby wanted when he wanted it. But somehow in these daily chores, interrupted constantly by unanticipated challenges, my husband and I hoped to raise a young man with values and competencies, not just a basket of wailing needs. Alignment or managing strategically means that all the things we do and the plans we make, through disruptions, surprises, and detours, come together for an awesome outcome.

Thirty-six years later I held my two-day-old granddaughter who slept contentedly in the cradle of my arms. Our tranquility was broken by a cold, hard thermometer jammed under her little arms with regularity. The baby's temperature jumped around quite a bit, and we would undertake the corresponding adjustments: swaddle looser, tighter; remove the hat, put on the hat; take off the socks, put the socks back on.

Ironically, large organizations are like babies. They too need sensors, monitors, assessments, and actions. In fact, organizations are even more needy than babies. Thousands of signals need to be tracked continuously. Some of these are lost, some are noted as disjointed readings, while others are monitored and interpreted by people dispersed functionally and geographically. Unlike babies, organizations do not come with built-in connectivity, flows, and central operating systems. All these must be put in place.

Alignment addresses coherence of the parts in adaptation to the environment for the success of the enterprise. The chief executive or executive director is the only person with the vantage point of the entire organization and oversight to direct every aspect of the entity. He or she is the person charged to care for the whole.

Broadly speaking, three types of coherence determine the effectiveness of an organization.

The first is the alignment between the external environment and the enterprise. External forces are not subject to the control of the organization but have significant impact on its viability. These forces include economic drivers of supply and demand and macro trends relating to national growth, inflation, wages, income distribution, costs of money, and so forth. Political forces shape government policies, regulation, funding, safety nets, public services, foreign policies, and the like. Social and cultural trends include demographics that define the needs of the population, expectations, norms, stability, lifestyles, cohesiveness, and so on. On the technology front innovations enter the mainstream of society and shape the way people work, live, communicate, heal, travel, recreate, and more.

Climate change is now recognized as a highly destructive force brought about by human action. The behavior of organizations will be scrutinized, through increasingly rigorous disclosure requirements, for their contribution to the problem of rising emissions and devastation or to solutions toward a green and inclusive economy.

As these forces evolve and play out, they affect the relevance, efficiency, and legitimacy of organizations. Through the thicket of external forces and challenges, organizations must find their path in a sequence of reinforcing next steps. These depend on what makes the most sense for organizations given their mission, purpose, strengths, weaknesses, investments, and competences.

Leaders need to forge a future from what they have, not from what they wish they had. Their decisions include the choice of products and services, which segments to serve; what programs to retain, terminate, and create; and the basis for achieving a distinctive advantage. Achieving alignment between the external and the internal is the work of strategic management.

The second type of coherence relates to the alignment of internal operations within the organization. Chief executives are like architects as they review the "fit for use" of the configuration of internal elements. Success comes from systematic implementation of strategy through coordinated functions and coherent structures. Alignment also contributes to the quality of the work environment by providing support, appropriate resources, clarity of expectations, and connectedness among the different parts of the organization. Coherence enhances personal and organizational success and contributes to the vitality of the organization.

Organizations are generally experienced in setting up functions replete with job descriptions and areas of responsibility. But they are frequently deficient in bringing about connectivity or integration between functions. Job descriptions tend not to include the responsibility for connectivity. Overall, there is no organizational manual for how this is done or who should do this. Unless alignment is managed explicitly, systematically, and energetically, it does not exist to the level needed.

When there is a leadership vacuum, alignment may evolve around a strong function or a strong functional leader. This may or may not serve the whole. The lack of strong connectivity creates mixed signals, confusion, duplication, gaps, backtracking, and delays. Energy is expended on internal issues rather than serving the beneficiaries or innovating to meet external challenges. The worst cases result in people intentionally or unintentionally working against one another.

Most leaders eschew the "c" word: control. It evokes image of behavior that is harsh, domineering, repressive, dogmatic, and authoritarian. But leaders need to shift their frame of reference to the consequences when organizations are out of control. In these contexts, people cannot do their work productively, and they don't reap success for themselves or for the enterprise. Organizations with weak controls are breeding grounds for fraud and other misbehavior.

The third type of coherence does not require skill. It requires character: the alignment between words and actions.

Employees operate within the culture of an organization. While not formalized into a department with its own personnel and reporting lines, culture reflects the operative values, norms, and rules people employ in regulating their behavior. Employees read signals and conclude: "Here, we win at all costs," "Here, we do not play with the numbers," "Here, we act and then ask for permission," "Here, we never stick our neck out," or "Here, we do what we can for the customers first."

Of all the signals they read, the ones they pay the most attention to are those of the leader. While integrity is expected of all employees, the printed mission and value statements have no purchase unless lived by the top leader. The leader's character is the organization's destiny.

Overall, the absence of alignment results in organizations where gears are not connected to leverage each other, where the collective outcome is not necessarily relevant to the people being served, and where words bear no influence on actions. Leaders make the difference on the level of coherence or disjointedness. While others can be enlisted for the task, the responsibility for alignment is that of the leader and cannot be delegated.

9

Capacity for Christian Witness

That the church is not an NGO (nongovernmental organization) was noted by Pope Francis on the first day of his papacy. He asked: "If we do not confess to Christ, what would we be?" And his answer: "We would end up a compassionate NGO. What would happen would be like when children make sand castles and then it all falls down."[1]

Pope Benedict XVI makes a similar point in *Deus Caritas Est*:

> With regard to the personnel who carry out the Church's charitable activity on the practical level, the essential has already been said: they must not be inspired by ideologies aimed at improving the world, but should rather be guided by the faith which works through love (cf. Gal 5:6). Consequently, more than anything, they must be persons moved by Christ's love, persons whose hearts Christ has conquered with his love, awakening within them a love of neighbor. The criterion inspiring their activity should be Saint Paul's statement in the Second Letter to the Corinthians: "the love of Christ urges us on" (5:14). The consciousness that,

---

[1] "Pope Francis Warns Church Could Become 'Compassionate NGO,'" *BBC News*, March 14, 2013.

in Christ, God has given himself for us, even unto death, must inspire us to live no longer for ourselves but for him, and, with him, for others. (no. 33)

Technically, the church is an NGO. The declaration by both pontiffs points to something else that defines the essence of the church: God's love and presence. The church is not just one more humanitarian organization undertaking good works to help others. Its works emanate from God's unconditional love for us. We serve from our encounter with God as witness of God's presence in the world here and now. Our work is a continuation of God's work. It is our response to the call of Christ to Peter to feed and tend his sheep. The church was born on Pentecost when the Holy Spirit descended on the apostles so that they could go out and make God known. With the Holy Spirit, we write our chapters of this love story.

This witness is not to proselytize or impose Catholic doctrine on others. It is the manifestation of love, the love of the ecclesial community, the love that points to God. As God loves all, we too are to love all without distinctions of creed, race, nationality, status, and so on. We try to love as God loves. This is the good news delivered in our work.

As the poem often attributed to St. Teresa of Avila states, we not only continue Christ's work but we work as his hands and feet, as his body in the world.

> Christ has no body but yours,
> No hands, no feet on earth but yours,
> Yours are the eyes with which he looks compas-
>   sion on this world.
> Yours are the feet with which he walks to do
>   good.
> Yours are the hands with which he blesses all
>   the world.

> Yours are the hands, yours are the feet, yours are
> the eyes, you are his body.

In the brothers and sisters we serve we are to see God, recognizing him in all people (Mt 25). Their dignity emanates from God. They are whole persons, not mere manifestations of hunger, poverty, sickness, abandonment, injustice, and violence. We may use our problem-solving skills, but people in need are not problems to be solved; rather, they are invitations to help build the kingdom of God. When we stand before them, we are on holy ground, because we stand before God. Our service helps not only them but places us on our own path of salvation. Service is gift. Catholic ministries deserve leaders who know they act from and in this grace.

Ministering to the people God entrusts to us calls for our very, very best. So often, people in Catholic ministries have settled for less than their full potential. Reasons cited: they do not have the resources to hire the best; their people do not have the expertise to take on new approaches; they have "done it this way" for a long time; the church cannot afford training and development; they need to wait until someone retires. With such rationalizations we put ourselves first. Our desires, approaches, fears, limitations, and job security define the parameters within which we reach out to the people who need us.

At CRS, I am reminded that our beneficiaries do not get waves of helpers and assistance. They get us. They get whatever level game we bring. Are we worthy of them? When they pray to God, God sends us as God's answer. Do we stand in awe of this privilege?

So often we clutch our ministries tightly to ourselves and carry the church's weary burdens by ourselves. It is easy to fall into deep worry about how much depends on us. Many ministry leaders work long hours, give up vacations, survive on few hours of sleep, and fall away from friends and hobbies. When

exhaustion drives out joy and perspectives, we have isolated ourselves and our work from God. A story about Pope John XXIII
recounts how he would go to bed each night noting to God:
"I've done the best I could in your service this day, O Lord. I'm
going to bed. It's your church. Take care of it!"

Hope is integral to the attitude of those leading faith-based
ministries. We hope not because we can see how everything unfolds according to our plans, and how we can execute as close to
perfection as possible. We recognize that God is in this work also.
We cannot see God's plans when things do not go well by our
standards or when we inadvertently mess things up. God makes
good out of all efforts. Good seeds planted for love will yield
good fruits. We may not see this in our lifetime or to our own
satisfaction. Hope takes over when we are sufficiently humble to
know we do not determine the outcome. My screensaver reads,
"Let go. Let God."

I have seen "letting go" result in acts of generosity that run
counter to the human impulse of holding on. About thirty years
ago healthcare was becoming more complex and difficult in all
dimensions (political, social, technological, financial). Different
religious orders of women who owned health systems recognized
that individually they did not have the scale and resources to
sustain the quality and scope of ministries to the poor.

One logical business response would be to sell the ministries.
Some did this. But other groups of religious sisters came together
to contribute their ministries, some formed over a hundred
years ago, to create a new entity that would have the where-
withal to not only survive but flourish. They would turn over
the ownership and governance of these hospitals to form a new
ministry which could sustain the vision and mission of Catholic
healthcare. These decisions were not made to recover financial
investments or achieve economic gains, but to ensure that the
healing ministry of Christ continues in a world that needs it
desperately. One such example is Ascension Health, formed in

1999 from the ministries of the Daughters of Charity and the Sisters of St. Joseph.

CRS under my predecessor, Ken Hackett, decided to give away its micro banks. CRS had developed micro-lending operations to assist smallholders, fishermen, and small entrepreneurs. These entities provided loans without oppressive interest rates. These micro banks had developed well and achieved viability and stability. They no longer needed the expertise of CRS staff and would be great additions to the local dioceses. Transferring ownership to the local church would enhance its financial strength and ability to serve the community.

During the meeting for one of these transfers, I met with the local bishop. I was quite concerned that the bishop would forgive all loans out of compassion. This pattern would not be optimal for the bank, the borrowers who needed to learn financial accountability, or even the diocese. So I ventured to comment: "Your excellency, I know it is necessary for you to forgive loans sometimes. But do not forgive all loans because the bank would collapse." He responded with great humor and humility: "Dr. Woo, I take your advice to heart. I would engage in careful discernment and tell people 'You know, I am trained to forgive sins, but I am not trained to forgive loans.'" It was a moment of warm conviviality and of the universal church in action. We know the Holy Spirit is behind the courage to let go, to trust, and to act from a different understanding of possession.

We pray fervently to God to help us in our work. But it is actually God's work, of which we are given a part. When the people needed food, Jesus asked what the disciples could do with the two loaves and five fishes. In this exchange he made them a part of the solution. What they brought, he multiplied. Divine multiplication was one of the first lessons I learned at CRS.

At mass one day, the gospel reading recounted the healing of the man lowered on a mat from the roof by his friends to seek Jesus's healing. When he picked up his mat and walked on his own, the people remarked, "We have seen remarkable things today" (Lk 5:26). Well, earlier that day I had just seen something similar: People who were close to death picked themselves up; they did not walk, they danced.

This happened at a village where folks with HIV/AIDS had gathered to celebrate. They were dressed in flowing white robes and dresses. They looked like angels. They marched in triumphant chorus clapping, swaying, ululating, and beating their drums. The antiretroviral treatments had restored their energy; they were able to plant, harvest, and sell nutritious sweet potatoes. Husbands and wives learned new ways to create the vision, habits, and commitment for a more loving marriage. The stigma they faced in the village was turning to acceptance and almost envy for their success. They were waiting for death before these interventions. Now they rejoined life with wonder and praise.

Repeatedly, I feel the bounty of God at work. There were malnourished children who at two years old weighed less than twenty pounds. They were nursed back to health with a regimen of highly nutritious food and supplements. When they ran around chasing one another and the chickens, I can hear God say, "This is how it should be."

We offered training and start-up resources that help women in very poor communities develop livelihood options so that they can feed and educate their children. One group gained access to water, allowing them to stay healthy and plant crops. They welcomed me into their simple homes, each displaying a picture of the Blessed Mother, with fresh pine needles that scented my path. Another group was led by a woman who was breastfeeding her child after losing an earlier baby to starvation because she herself had no food.

Sure, there are modern medicine, gifts of seeds and money, creative programming, and devoted staff. These are not separate from God, but are God's gifts and endowments to us: intelligence, inventiveness, goodness, dedication. As Pope Benedict XVI taught in *Deus Caritas Est,* it is the human instinct to love, but that instinct is placed in us by God. These somehow come together in unbelievable ways to beat the odds. Christian witness is to hold in trust that we may do the work, but the rest is up to God. We sow, and God sends the nourishment and the harvest. We work with and in God. In this light, our works are holy.

Through prayer, we cultivate mindfulness for God. Quite a few of our women leaders cite the centrality of prayer in their work. In prayer, we explicitly place ourselves in the presence of God. Attention, as Simone Weil notes, is prayer. We make room for God's ways and God's will. We channel God's grace. In prayer, our women leaders find guidance, strength, consolation, renewal, and peace.

It is not enough for Catholic ministry leaders to operate with this sense of God in themselves. As heads of their institutions, they also have a responsibility to embed this in the mission, priorities, values, and culture of the institution. Their witness is not a personal or private matter; it needs to be the drumbeat and tuning fork for their organizations. Catholic ministry exists for the witness of God's presence and love in this world here and now. We work in God's name to meet concrete and real needs with our special expertise. We support the dignity of all people, particularly those who are most vulnerable. Love for neighbors as embodied in Catholic social teaching becomes the guiding principle and guardrail for institutions' decisions, policies, and behavior.

In this responsibility, leaders are akin to elders who uphold the identity and heritage of the community. Through teaching and modeling in storytelling, rituals, and symbols, the elders keep this identity vibrant and relevant. The elders pass on this mantle and prepare the next generation to understand what it is, why it is important, and how to bring it to life in an ever-changing milieu. Future leaders cannot infuse mission with passion and commitment if they do not cherish it; they cannot cherish it if they do not know it; they cannot know it if it is not taught; and mission can only be taught through proclamation and actions.

We act from this witness in engaging the external world. In our relationships with stakeholders, we must be clear that we act humbly in the name of God. Our work is governed by a set of principles that honors human dignity and promotes flourishing of the whole person. People should know us by our adherence to these principles and understand what Catholicism stands for by our actions. In many of the non-Christian countries CRS works in, proselytizing is forbidden. We do not teach God; we manifest God.

I have participated in quite a number of board discussions pertaining to the search for a new president or executive director for a Catholic ministry. Does the person have to be a practicing Catholic?

Search consultants and board members inevitably note that many people among non-Catholics and non-Christians understand Catholic social teaching and are drawn to it. They too are inspired to serve the poor and vulnerable according to the principles of solidarity, subsidiarity, rights of labor, respect for life and family, and care for our common home. In sectors such as healthcare and higher education where well-rounded talent is in short supply, the sentiment often leans to finding the most competent candidate who also respects Catholic values.

I think this misses the point. Catholic ministries are not just NGOs, as the two popes teach. These are more than goodhearted organizations doing goodhearted work. Priority one for Catholic ministries is to manifest God through the organized institutional expressions of the ecclesial community. We seek not only economic and social justice, but holiness. Can leaders profess God? Locate themselves in God? Work with and in the power of the Holy Spirit? Can they call forth, inspire, and teach colleagues to carry out this mission? Is this optional? What is Catholic ministry without Christian witness?

PART III

JOURNEYS OF LEADERSHIP IN CATHOLIC MINISTRIES

10

Betsy Bohlen

Chief Operating Officer, Archdiocese of Chicago, Illinois

Elizabeth (Betsy) Bohlen is the chief operating officer of the Archdiocese of Chicago, where she oversees all administrative operations and brings strategic planning, organization, and implementation expertise to strategic pastoral initiatives. She joined the archdiocese in 2011 after many years of involvement through pro bono consulting engagement and as a member of the Archdiocesan Finance Council. Prior to the archdiocese, Ms. Bohlen was a partner at McKinsey & Company, an international management consulting firm. She has also served as an investment officer for the Slovak American Enterprise Fund in Bratislava, Slovakia, and a financial analyst at the First Boston Corporation (now Credit Suisse), a global investment bank. Ms. Bohlen holds a master of business administration degree from Harvard Business School. She received her bachelor of arts in economics, with a minor in theology, from the University of Notre Dame. Ms. Bohlen lives in the Hyde Park neighborhood of Chicago with her husband, Jon, and their two children.

On most days I would say I have found myself working in an unexpected setting. In other ways, though, my path was written in my heart all along.

I am currently the chief operating officer of the Archdiocese of Chicago, a role that is relatively new in archdiocesan structures, supporting the archbishop in managing archdiocesan initiatives and operations.

In any given day I focus time and effort on the full range of our priorities: fostering the effectiveness of our parishes and schools, building the functional capabilities needed to address our challenges, ensuring strong stewardship of our financial resources, working to build a Christ-centered and effective organizational culture in our Pastoral Center, and perhaps most important, adding my particular skills to our spiritual renewal efforts.

My Vocational Calling

In retrospect, my discernment for this role began at the end of my undergraduate years at the University of Notre Dame. I was trying to reconcile a dedication to my faith with what seemed to be an incongruous desire to accept a position at a Wall Street investment bank. A priest professor helped me understand then that vocations come in many flavors, and that I might be discerning a calling to be a Christian witness in the business world. I joined the Wall Street firm. During those two years at the investment bank, I came to understand better my heart's desire to develop business skills, and the care and community that can flourish in any workplace. By the time I entered business school for my MBA two years later, I had discerned a two-pronged path to my career: first, that I would serve out a vocation in the business world while also developing important skills, and second, that one day I would use those skills in the service of some not-for-profit mission.

After my business school graduation I joined a leading management consulting firm to develop strategy, organization, and management skills, particularly for large and complex institutions. I enjoyed the work, serving clients and working with many exceptional people. During that time I also volunteered on a number of pro bono projects, applying the skills I was developing to the problems of a range of not-for-profit institutions. I did this for its own sake, but also to explore areas of possible interest in some possible future career.

One pro bono engagement, and one airplane flight, really stood out. I had started to serve the Archdiocese of Chicago. On a long flight home one day I had two projects to focus on: a reasonably interesting strategy engagement for a corporate client, and a mundane process improvement pro bono effort for the archdiocese. During that flight I was surprised by a very strong pull to work on the archdiocesan process effort that, in any other circumstance, I would find much less interesting than the strategy engagement. I knew then that I was experiencing a deep call to serve the church in a more meaningful way.

Over the next several years I mostly tried to answer this call my own way—dedicating volunteer time to the archdiocese, particularly when I was taking a break from full-time work while we had young children at home. I convinced myself, often, that I was following that calling by engaging in these ways, but deep down I always knew I was being asked to give more of myself. I finally took a sabbatical from my consulting firm to help the archdiocese for one year starting in 2011. I decided to continue to serve after my sabbatical ended, and, in 2014, the newly ap-pointed archbishop, Blase Cupich, created the position of chief operating officer of the archdiocese, asking me to serve in that capacity. I have been at the archdiocese ever since.

My Current Calling in the Church

We have been living through difficult times in the church. Most important, younger generations are simply walking away from a life of faith, with only 11 percent of children now raised Catholic growing into adults who practice their faith regularly. Declines in faith practice have spilled over into a crisis of vocations, a decline in Catholic school enrollment, depleted resources, unsustainable parish operations, and difficulties maintaining the beautiful churches bequeathed to us. We also have lost institutional trust and confidence because of the misconduct scandal.

Accordingly, my role often places me in the middle of difficult and painful topics. I recall one particular day early in my time at the archdiocese. In the morning I visited an empty convent to determine our options given its dilapidated state. I walked into the chapel, now unused and with leftover altar clothes strewn about, a stark contrast to the image in my head of that chapel when it was brimming with numerous religious sisters. At midday I attended a meeting during which we made the difficult decision to close some Catholic schools with low and unsustainable enrollment, schools that had once been filled with hundreds of Catholic schoolchildren. Finally, in the late afternoon, I was part of a group that reviewed the very difficult testimony of victims who had come forward about sexual abuse by a priest when they were younger.

Because of the loss of trust in institutions generally, and in the church in particular, I have also been surprised by the willingness of journalists and others to believe the worst about us on some topics, even when the facts suggest otherwise. Working to overcome misperceptions has too often consumed significant time.

Despite the difficulties, I see signs of God's presence and hope in the talented, dedicated people who come to serve the church during these times; in the commitment of priests, staff, and parishioners to renewal; in the care of God's people by our ministers even in these difficult times; in the service of our charities in helping people in need.

People often ask me how I managed to give up a business career to come serve the church, or how I manage to stick with my work given our challenges and the difficulties of trying to lead transformational change in a church setting. I know well that the fire that fuels me is not my own—it comes from the Holy Spirit and gives me a fervor and drive that I would not have on my own, supporting me in persevering through setbacks and difficulties. I have also come to learn that God does work in mysterious ways when it comes to whom God calls. I often believe I am not the best fit for this role—with too much of a "thinking style" rather than a "feeling style," and a harder-charging approach that can be overwhelming for others at times.

Over the years I have come to understand my role as "tilling the soil"—doing the cleanup and preparation now for some later fruitfulness that will mostly come after my lifetime. I have learned to become comfortable that the time horizon for renewal is not my own, and that even the way renewal will happen in God's plan might be very different from the one I might envision.

In all of my work I try to "pray as though everything depended on God and work as through everything depended on you" (a quotation ascribed either to St. Ignatius or St. Augustine), recognizing the need to discern and follow God's will.

Convictions That Ground My Work

These days I wake up each morning with the grace-filled drive to give all I have to our church because of three primary convictions:

Organizational skill matters for the church. Over the past century a new area of human skill has emerged, the management of large and complex institutions, as transformations in communications, transportation, and information have led to the development of large institutions. Some people devote significant training and long years of career development to grow in these skills, just as surgeons, lawyers, engineers, and priests devote significant training and time to developing in their chosen professions.

Any diocese or archdiocese is a complex operation that faces significant issues. The mission of the church can benefit from a range of organizational skills, such as strategy, priority setting, analysis, planning, team development, coordination, and process implementation. Importantly, not bringing these skills to address the level of complexity we face can lead to poor decisions, low impact, and harm to the mission of our church. I firmly believe that inadequate organizational skill is at the root of some of our most difficult and painful challenges in the church. I see many signs of hopefulness as bishops and archbishops begin to explore the organizational support they need to be effective shepherds of their local churches. I am also consistently heartened by the extent to which very talented people with organizational and administrative backgrounds are willing to contribute to the mission of our church.

Our parish model must transform to reintroduce Christ to the world. Our parish model makes many implicit assumptions that no longer hold: that our surrounding culture is supportive of faith, that faith practice and formation within families are strong, and that people come into our parishes already knitted together by strong ethnic and/or neighborhood ties. While these assumptions no longer hold, I am energized by a vision for parish renewal we have been developing in the Archdiocese of Chicago with five core themes: compelling *entry points* by which people can encounter Christ and explore a life of faith from the beginning (Is there a God? Who is Christ? Why does the church matter?); *radical hospitality* that welcomes all who come and brings them into a deep community otherwise usually missing in today's secular world; *vibrant worship* of strong and participatory liturgies, homilies, and music; *readiness-based formation* that meets everyone where they are in faith formation; and *outreach and charity* that intentionally go out to seek the lost.

Christ is the answer to our country's ailing, and people are longing for Christ's healing. Statistics show skyrocketing trends in loneliness, despair, and drug addiction. These are rooted in a search for meaning outside of God's grace and love as revealed through Christ. Our imperative is to recommit now in significant ways to inviting people and creating open space for reencountering God. Our parish renewal efforts are more important than ever.

The Pastoral Center at the Archdiocese of Chicago has a beautiful Gothic courtyard, and I often walk through it on my way into the building, pondering what has become of my calling to serve our church. Many days have been difficult indeed, but there have also been many days of rejoicing and hopefulness. I am honored to have been called to serve the church in the Archdiocese of Chicago; I am grateful for the support and collaboration of our archbishops, bishops, team members, and volunteer council members; and I am thankful to be part of a day-to-day team deeply committed to serving the church in these times.

11

Sister Simone Campbell, SSS

(Retired) Executive Director, NETWORK, Washington, DC

Simone Campbell, SSS, is a Sister of Social Service, attorney, and poet. Simone has had a varied career. She practiced law for eighteen years, serving working families' needs in Oakland, California. Her community members elected Simone to be their leader for the term 1995–2000. She had the honor of leading her Sisters in the United States, Mexico, Taiwan, and the Philippines. After a sabbatical Simone led Jericho, an interfaith California public-policy organization in Sacramento, California. From 2004 until 2021 she was the executive director of NETWORK, a lobby for Catholic social justice based in Washington, DC. NETWORK lobbies for policies that will mend the income and wealth gaps in our nation and create racial equity in this challenging time. As leader of NETWORK, Simone led seven Nuns on the Bus trips across the country, each one advocating for a different social justice need in our nation. She spoke at the Democratic National Convention in 2012 and 2020, appeared on numerous radio and television news shows, and received numerous awards. She is the author of *A Nun on the Bus* (HarperOne, 2014) and *Hunger for Hope* (Orbis Books, 2020).

◇◇◇◇◇◇◇◇◇◇◇◇◇◇◇◇

I have an early primal memory that probably begins from when I was about eighteen months old. My dad would kiss me goodbye before going to work and say something to the effect of "Be a good girl and take care of your mom and baby sister." I took him seriously. This admonition has shaped me all these years. It shaped me in being responsible and responding to the needs around me. It also instilled in me early on a sense of capacity to affect others. I do not know if he intended such a result, but this is what happened.

It resulted in me being the organizer of some events in the neighborhood. We (the neighborhood gaggle of kids) put on plays for our mothers for Mother's Day in our backyard in our southern California tract house. We had a "demonstration" in favor of Proposition 3 (whatever that was). We made yarn dolls and sold them to raise money for an outing we wanted. It seemed that my sister, Katy, and I were at the center of the creativity and the action.

My mom stayed home with us in the 1950s while my dad went to work. We saw her help out at school as a substitute teacher and creating extracurricular activities like sewing. In third grade my class had a terrible teacher who only called on a few students, including me. This seemed wrong to me. I thought everyone should be involved, so I wrote a Thanksgiving play that included the entire class. I wanted to demonstrate that all could and should star in some way. In a sign of affirmation for such ingenuity, the faculty saw that we put it on for the whole school. We did another play at Easter time, again for the whole school. My parents and faculty supported such endeavors.

I also saw my parents make choices that were "outside the lines" of what were then the regulations. When I started elementary school, our parish, Our Lady of Refuge, did not have a Catholic school. My parents sent me to St. Bartholomew's School in the neighboring parish. When I was going into third grade and my sister into first, our parish opened a school with

Sisters from Ireland. My parents decided to keep us at St. Bartholomew's. This was very much against the norms of the time. My mom used to refer to us as the "refugees," both as the name of our parish and the fact that we had "fled." I learned both humor and coloring outside the lines.

When I was a senior in high school and my sister, Katy, was a sophomore, she was diagnosed with Hodgkin's disease and given three to five years to live. It is difficult to explain in a few words how this affected our family on so many levels. Katy lived for five years and died when she was a junior in college. I have come to realize that in some ways I have picked up her life as well as my own and lived with an intensity that reflects her passion as well as mine. But this insight has only come in my middle years thanks to both a contemplative practice and therapy.

After my freshman year in college I was eager to get on with life and tired of being in a classroom. I joined my religious community, the Sisters of Social Service. My community was founded in Budapest, Hungary, in 1923. Our foundress, Margaret Slachta, was the first woman in the Hungarian Parliament when she was the leader of our community. Our Sisters did social work in a time when Sisters were cloistered, teachers and nurses. We did not wear elaborate habits and in fact called our gray street-length dresses a uniform. We lived together in community and went out to our individual ministries. I knew our Sisters from the girls camp that my sister and I attended. It was a high point of our year. I was drawn to the energy and activism of the community in the 1960s. In our three years of formation I learned about our dedication to the Holy Spirit and the beginnings of a contemplative practice.

After first profession our leadership assigned us to our ministries. While this might seem strange, I have come to realize that our Sister leaders assigned us to ministries that we would not have aspired to ourselves. They saw more gifts in us than we saw in ourselves. They assigned us with this vision of our capacity and not our feelings of inadequacy. My first full-time assignment (after finishing my BA with full-time study and part-time work) was as the Oregon Archdiocese's religious education consultant for non-school religious education. At the age of twenty-three I traveled western Oregon doing teacher training, creating programs, integrating social justice into religious education. It was a glorious ministry as I was pushed into the deep end of responsibility and opportunity. I still have many friends from that time of growth and discovery.

During my time in Portland, I discovered a calling to go to law school. I was a volunteer in a community-organizing project and discovered I hated a power imbalance. If I was going to do this sort of policy work, I needed to understand the law. It was dazzlingly clear to me. One of the Sisters I lived with was a tremendous help when she raised the fact that none of our Sisters had gone to law school. Everyone was a social worker. She got me to write my first "brief," setting out how such a career path fit our mission and charism. I recently learned that she was worried that my dreams would be crushed by our leadership and was trying to soften the blow. Her contribution resulted in my "arguing my case" and getting the approval to go to law school.

I went to the University of California at Davis law school to do public policy but discovered that I like practicing law. After graduation, I set up a low-cost legal service center to serve the working poor who did not qualify for free legal service but could not afford private counsel. We ended up doing all of the high-conflict, low-income family law cases in our county. Being a member of my community allowed me to respond to unmet social needs. My Sisters were willing to support me in community until we were established and could pay some salary. By the time I left eighteen years later, we were six attorneys, six paralegals, and other support staff.

One of the gifts of the law center was the fact that it coincided with the evolution of the Family Law Court in Alameda

County. We were in on the ground floor of the creation of Family Court Services for mediation in custody/visitation cases. I did not use my title Sister in the practice of law, because it seemed to me to create confusion for clients and at times for opposing counsel. However, it got out that I was a Catholic Sister when one of the judges found out. So the members of the bench and bar knew, but not many of my clients. However, I believe that this knowledge helped me be a leader in the family law community and advocate for the needs of low-income litigants. Additionally, I learned a Christian Zen practice that became the anchor of my spiritual life. I experienced it as "deep listening to the Spirit."

When I left the law center, I thought that I would start something new to respond to the needs of working families. However, I was elected to be the leader of my international community. It was my most challenging leadership position. But my Sisters taught me to speak of my spiritual journey and to continue to anchor myself in the contemplative practice. They did this through their criticism and my taking the criticisms that hurt to my contemplative practice until I knew the truth that hurt. The most painful anguish was their criticism that I was too corporate. Finally, I learned the truthful insight that I was not really corporate. Rather, the truth was that my lawyerly style was all that my Sisters saw because I was not sharing my spiritual journey. They taught me to integrate talking about my spiritual practice into my work of service.

Following my five years in leadership and a glorious sabbatical, I began to do the work that led me to go to law school in the first place. First, I was hired as the executive director of a California interfaith advocacy organization started by one of my Sisters. I learned the ropes of lobbying and the needs of California. Because of my leadership, we advocates tried to connect with our new governor, Arnold Schwarzenegger. We were unsuccessful in that effort, but the attempt led to our having quarterly meetings with his secretary of health and human services. It gave us a chance to express the needs of all Californians and to make a difference in administrative policy. This structured meeting continued after I was recruited to come to Washington, DC, and NETWORK.

NETWORK lobbies on Capitol Hill for economic and social transformation. Our almost fifty-year-old organization was founded to create systemic change by networking together Catholic Sisters from across the country. The key to leadership for me has been a contemplative practice of "deep listening" to the Spirit. My experience is that the Spirit has continued to lead as we created a critical letter in support of the Affordable Care Act (ACA) signed by fifty-nine leaders of Catholic Sisters' communities. My Sisters signed on even though the US Conference of Catholic Bishops had come out opposing the bill. This letter was the tipping point in the passage of the ACA.

Two years later, we were celebrating NETWORK's fortieth anniversary and the question was raised: What can we do to let people know that we have been lobbying on Capitol Hill for forty years?

Four days later the Vatican answered our prayer when it issued a reprimand of the Leadership Conference of Women Religious (LCWR) and named our little organization as being a bad influence on Catholic Sisters. My prayer became: How do we use this moment for our mission? I was led to ask for the help of our secular colleagues, and it resulted in our first Nuns on the Bus campaign. It was an explosion of energy opposing a draconian federal budget proposed by Congressman Paul Ryan. We never said a word about the Vatican action; we just stayed true to our mission and used the shadow of the controversy to draw attention to this need.

We have now done seven Nuns on the Bus trips across our country speaking out on various justice issues. This has led to a heightened notoriety and effectiveness in our advocacy. I have come to describe my spirituality as "walking willing" or "walking toward trouble." I have learned that the needs of our people break my heart. When I am focused on their needs, nothing stops me. It is a continuing Pentecost of the movement of the Spirit. Focus on the needs of others is the source of movement and change. How can I shy away when others are in need?

I have never set out to be a leader in the church. In fact, I do not consider myself a leader in the church and resisted this project. Rather, I consider myself as a leader who strives to take the gospel to where it would not be otherwise. I live the Pentecost reality of "go forth." I try to respond to the mandate to share the fire of the Spirit by being open to having my heart broken open. And with a broken heart walk toward the need and the potential healing. It is the echo of my dad's admonition: Take care of your mother and your sister.

12

Cyril Cruz

Principal, Holy Innocents School, Long Beach, California

Cyril Cruz is a wife, mother of six, and principal of Holy Innocents Catholic Classical School in Long Beach, California. Cyril has worked in the public sector for the Compton Unified School District as a middle-school science teacher and curriculum developer. She has also served in Catholic education as a teacher and now administrator for the Archdiocese of Los Angeles. She is honored and blessed to be serving the families of Holy Innocents School with the mission to form their children for sainthood.

I am a cradle Catholic who grew up in a family that did not practice the faith. I am a first-generation child of Filipino immigrants. My father served for the United States Navy for thirty years, and my mother worked in healthcare for Long Beach Memorial Medical Center for twenty-five years.

I am a product of a public school education. My saving grace was my middle-school best friend, Gina Carmolinga, and her mother, Sylvia Carmolinga. Mama Sylvia opened me up to the Catholic faith with her invitation to join the confirmation

program at St. Lucy Catholic Church. At St. Lucy I was formed
as a youth leader through the youth group and catechesis programs. I was a youth minister and a CCD and confirmation
teacher.

At St. Lucy I was introduced to the missionary order Oblate
Apostles of the Two Hearts (OATH). The order taught me the
importance of reverence of the Most Holy Eucharist, honor of
the Blessed Virgin Mary, and practice of praying for the salvation
of souls. My spiritual life continued to be formed throughout
my high school and college years by the OATH. I was able to
travel to different countries giving talks to youth and young
adults about the importance of clinging to the sacraments and
the importance of having a good relationship with Christ.

I graduated from Long Beach Polytechnic High School in
2000 with hopes of going into the medical field. I was blessed
to use my dad's VA benefits to attend public college for free. I
started in the nursing field and quickly became interested in
biology. I transferred to California State University Long Beach,
where I majored in biology and physiology with a minor in
chemistry. I was given the opportunity to do research in a com-
parative muscle physiology laboratory.

With graduation around the corner, I started discerning my
next steps, whether to continue with research or move forward
in the medical field. I started to research the requirements for
physician assistant school. I took classes at Mount San Antonio
College and started shadowing a physician assistant in the city
of South Gate. Her clinic served a population of primarily low-
income and Hispanic people. Her care for patients taught me the
importance of the dignity of the person and the gift of listening.
This experience vaulted me into really discerning another option
in the sciences. My spiritual director suggested that because of
my love for Christ and teaching youth and my love for science,
I should pray about becoming an educator.

I must also insert that early in my college years I made very good friends, Catholic young adults who were very inspirational and better Catholics than I was. They pushed me to strive for holiness. They kept me accountable in my school studies and work. My husband, Michael, was a huge part of this formation. Our courtship and service together in the church were a strong foundation for our marriage. My prayer life existed because of Michael. Our courtship started in 2000, our first year of college. In 2004, my husband wanted to discern a religious calling. This was one of the most difficult times for me. We broke off our relationship, and he entered seminary.

As a young adult yearning for purpose and a deeper relationship with Christ, I found the adoration chapel at Sts. Peter and Paul in Wilmington, California, where Fr. Peter Irving III was the parish priest. His love of the Eucharist and the Blessed Mother and zeal for souls was inspiring and exactly what my soul and heart needed. I was attending daily mass, praying in front of the Blessed Sacrament for one to two hours a day, praying four Rosaries a day, doing spiritual reading, and journaling. This difficult time turned into the most peaceful and consoling period of my life. God was ordering my life, and I was listening. After discernment, Michael left the seminary. We eventually restarted our courtship, both of us different persons, with a strong and prayerful disposition.

Upon graduation from CSULB in 2006, I decided to enroll in a master of education program through the University of Phoenix. I was immediately pushed into my first job as teacher through student teaching. I started working at Bunche Middle School in the Compton Unified School District. I was hired as the seventh-grade life science teacher. My first day I was given a curriculum map, pacing guide, and teacher edition book. I did not have any professional teaching experience and was literally thrown into the classroom. I learned quickly through my colleagues and program. At Bunche Middle School I became close friends with my administrator, Dr. Michael Nkemnji, and Mrs. Susan Smith, a fellow teacher, both vibrant practicing Christians who offered much solace in prayer and encouragement.

In 2008, I married Michael and started having children. I completed my master's in secondary education and remained at Bunche for the next five years. My family was growing. In 2012, I had three daughters and was pregnant with our first son. At Bunche, I created curriculum and assessments for the district in an effort to raise test scores and provide a better education for our students. In 2012, the district introduced a sex-education program that was to be taught to our seventh graders. This sent me into major discernment regarding my vocation as teacher and even greater regarding my vocation as wife and mother. My oldest daughter was going to be starting school, and my husband and I discerned the possibility of homeschooling. We decided to homeschool, but that decision was very short lived. Due to a change in pay and title at my husband's job, I needed to start looking for another job.

One day at mass Fr. Peter approached me and asked if I wanted to teach at Holy Innocents School. There was an opening for a second-grade teacher. I was in awe at the miracle and quickly accepted. My daughter was able to receive the Catholic education that I never experienced. Catherine entered TK (transitional kindergarten), and I went into second grade. God really does provide. My principal the first year was Sr. Mary Elizabeth, OCD. She was a great formator and spiritual mother. The transition from public middle school to private second grade was difficult. My colleagues were the best examples of Catholic teachers in and out of the classroom. Their witness of their vocation to married, single, and religious life was inspirational. A few stand-out mentors are Mrs. Jessica McFadden, Mrs. Araceli Delas Armas, Mr. Gary Page, and Mrs. Joan Mullins. My first group of students and their families taught me the importance of my own witness to the faith.

At Holy Innocents I taught second grade twice, then seventh, eighth, sixth, and third grades. For years our school had been underperforming on standardized tests. Our faulty attended specific training from the archdiocese to examine curriculum and teaching methods to raise test scores. But these efforts were not successful.

In 2017, our pastor, Fr. Peter, introduced our faculty to the beautiful world of the Catholic Classical Liberal Arts program. A decision was made to adopt this curriculum. With that decision the Carmelite Sisters decided to ask Fr. Peter to fund a person to help transition the school in the endeavor.

Through much discernment, I decided to apply for the position of principal, and I was chosen to serve. With guidance from the Institute for Catholic Liberal Education (ICLE) and colleagues like Mary Pat Donohue, Michael Van Hecke, Elisabeth Sullivan, Colleen Richards, Rosemary Vanderweele, Chris Weir, and many others, we are able to provide to our scholars a beautiful formation that is grounded in wisdom and virtue for the pursuit of the true, good, and beautiful. I feel incredibly honored, humbled, and blessed to be a part of this mission of forming souls for heaven.

13

Kim Daniels

Co-Director, Initiative on Catholic Social Thought and Public Life, Georgetown University, Washington, DC

Kim Daniels is the co-director of Georgetown University's Initiative on Catholic Social Thought and Public Life. She was appointed by Pope Francis as a member of the Vatican Dicastery for Communication in 2016 and has served as spokesperson for the president of the United States Conference of Catholic Bishops (USCCB). She currently serves as a consultor to the USCCB's Committee for Religious Liberty and has advised the USCCB and other Catholic institutions on a broad range of issues where church teachings intersect with public life, including immigration, human life and dignity, religious liberty, and care for creation. Kim is a graduate of Princeton University and the University of Chicago Law School and lives with her husband and children in Bethesda, Maryland.

◇◇◇◇◇◇◇◇◇◇◇◇◇◇◇◇

I spent a wet March afternoon in 2013 in St. Peter's Square waiting with so many others for the white smoke that would indicate that Catholics had a new pope. Pope Benedict XVI had unexpectedly resigned, and I had come to Rome to offer media commentary on the conclave that would elect Pope Francis.

That morning I'd gotten a call asking me to meet with Cardinal Timothy Dolan of New York to talk about serving as his spokesperson in his role as president of the USCCB. When the time came, I was waterlogged from the drizzle, and the heel on one of my shoes was about to give up the ghost to the cobblestoned streets. But as I walked up the hill to meet him, I was nothing but excited for this new opportunity.

It was the beginning of a new chapter in my professional life, completing a transition from legal work focused on religious liberty and pro-life issues to a broader role helping church leaders and institutions communicate more effectively about those and many other important issues at the intersection of faith and public life.

I had a real learning experience at the bishops' conference. I learned some of the ins-and-outs of working for a centuries-old institution of some 1.3 billion diverse people from around the world from people like Linda Hunt, who had been a leader at the conference for over two decades. I learned from subject-matter experts about the nuances of the broad range of issues central to the church's efforts in public life, including life and human dignity, responses to poverty, immigration, and care for creation. And I learned about church communications from professionals like Helen Osman and Sr. Mary Ann Walsh, two leaders in the field who brought experience, dedication, and professionalism to their work. Today I continue to serve the bishops' conference as a lay consultant to the Committee for Religious Liberty.

Like so many others, I've had to navigate a balance between work and family life, and after full-time work at the USCCB I shifted to consulting from home for the conference as well as for other Catholic institutions and ministries. One of my projects was as a lead member of the team responsible for the US introduction of *Laudato Si'*, Pope Francis's encyclical on the environment. Throughout this time I met many women exercising real leadership in the church, including Carolyn Woo, CEO of

Catholic Relief Services, and Joan Rosenhauer, CRS's executive vice president (and now the executive director of Jesuit Relief Services).

In July 2016 I added another role to the mix. My husband and I were staying with our large extended family at the New Jersey shore with our six children, and in the middle of shaking out sandy towels and talking about whether we should head to the boardwalk that night, I snuck a look at my email. There was one in Italian addressed to "Gentilissima Dott.ssa. Kim Daniels," and to be honest, I thought it was spam and almost deleted it. Fortunately I did a double take, ran it through Google Translate, and learned that Pope Francis had named me a member of the Vatican Secretariat (now Dicastery) for Communication.

I've continued in this role since then, and it's been an honor to serve the holy father and the church, and to work with the team at the Vatican in helping to communicate the goodness, truth, and beauty at the heart of our faith, not through "marketing and strategizing" but through "the beating heart of the gospel." Pope Francis calls us to live out our faith in these challenging times not by withdrawing into ourselves or retreating from the world, but through "witness in the first place," resisting fear and remembering that "the solution is not to draw our sword against others, or to flee from the times in which we live. The solution is the way of Jesus: active love, humble love, love 'to the end'" (Jn 13:1).

As part of those efforts I worked closely with the organizing committee of the February 2019 Vatican Meeting on the Protection of Minors in the Church, along with my friend Ann Carter, a consultor to the dicastery, a longtime adviser to Cardinal Sean O'Malley of Boston and a founder of a top Boston communications firm. This global summit of episcopal leaders was an important driver of several much-needed concrete reforms in the way the church responds to the clergy sexual-abuse crisis, and I was glad to play a small part in bringing it together, in particular by helping bring the voices of women and victim-survivors of clergy abuse to the center of the conversation.

In 2018, I joined my friend John Carr at Georgetown University's Initiative on Catholic Social Thought and Public Life, where we work to promote dialogue on Catholic social thought and national and global issues; build bridges across political, religious, and ideological lines; and encourage a new generation of Catholic lay leaders to see their faith as an asset in pursuing the common good. Just this year John and the university asked me to become the co-director of the initiative. We've found that there is a hunger for principled civil dialogue and for the moral vocabulary of Catholic social thought in our wounded church and divided nation. We've had many wonderful Catholic women leaders join us in these efforts, from Sr. Norma Pimentel of Catholic Charities of the Rio Grande Valley on the US-Mexico border to prominent Black Catholic pro-life leader Gloria Purvis.

Through all this time, I've learned from others' examples that it's vital for Catholic women to take on leadership roles in order for our church to bring an effective witness to our troubled world. Pope Francis offers a model for what such witness looks like, whatever our roles: lift up the gospel of Jesus Christ; offer humble service to our neighbors, especially the poor and vulnerable; and bring Catholic social principles to public life with mercy and generosity.

While I've had great opportunities, it hasn't always been easy. Clericalism is real and harmful. Like others, I've been dismissed or patronized or pigeonholed because of who I am or the views I hold—because I'm a woman, or because I'm a mom of six; because I support Pope Francis, or because of my background doing pro-life and religious liberty work. It's sometimes hard to explain my service to the institutional church to some of my students who think it too often doesn't treat women with equal respect. And seeing the clergy sex-abuse crisis up close has often been discouraging and dispiriting, particularly because it's clear that had more women been in the rooms where decisions were made, we wouldn't be where we are today.

But the broken body of Christ is still the body of Christ, the source of our joy and our hope. When I pray the Creed I believe every line is true, and I know that those truths, and the love in which they're grounded, unite Catholics as a family. I know that around the world the church still lives out our gospel mission—love of God and neighbor, especially those "lying wounded along the roadside"—every single day, celebrating the sacraments and caring for the sick and sheltering the homeless and serving the poor and vulnerable. Our church, as Pope Francis says, is a home with open doors, and I am grateful and humbled to be a part of it.

14

Jennifer Fiduccia

*Director of Leadership Consultants, Catholic
Leadership Institute, Malvern, Pennsylvania*

Jennifer Fiduccia has been an active member of the church since her teen years as a youth cantor and peer minister. Over twenty years she has worked in music ministry, youth and young adult ministry, adult formation, and with RCIA. She served as director of formation from 2011 to 2021 at St. Francis of Assisi Catholic Community in Raleigh, North Carolina. Jennifer earned her undergraduate degree in vocal performance from New York University, two graduate degrees in theological studies and catechetical ministry from the University of Dallas, and a certificate in church management from Villanova University. She sits on the Admissions and Scrutinies Committee for the Office of the Diaconate in the Diocese of Raleigh and has published liturgical music. In August 2021, Jenn accepted a new position as Director of Leadership Consultants at the Catholic Leadership Institute. With her husband, Pat, and four children, Jennifer enjoys camping, reading, writing music, and baking.

◇◇◇◇◇◇◇◇◇◇◇◇◇◇◇

"You, my dear, are not matronly enough." The pastor had casually tossed these words out in response to the idea that I could direct an upcoming women's retreat. I guess I should have been flattered as a young youth minister. Fourteen years and four kids later, I would certainly take it as a compliment! His comments, however, shed some light on my experience as a woman in a parish leadership role, holding in tension my gifts for and vocation to ministry with my identity as a woman and the limitations that can bring working for the church.

If you ask my mother, she will tell you that I had a penchant for being in charge and calling the shots at a young age. Apparently, I often treated my younger brother as an employee, and for one early holiday, I received a book from the then-popular *Mr. Men and Little Miss* series by Roger and Adam Hargreaves called *Little Miss Bossy*. (One of my favorite memes reads, "I'm not bossy, I'm aggressively helpful.") Time, education, good mentors, and a whole lot of help from the Spirit have helped me in channeling these tendencies, cultivating my giftedness into the charism of leadership.

Over the years I have found that my very presence as a young(ish), confident, visionary female in a leadership role is intimidating to some. I learned that certain colleagues feel threatened by me, especially men in higher levels of authority. Being in a leadership position can sometimes be lonely and alienating. Working for an organization that does not admit women into the highest levels of leadership has presented a particular challenge.

It was not my dream to be a lay ecclesial minister, but as I love to tell those that I work with in the RCIA, God draws straight with our crooked lines. Graduating high school, I had my sights set on law school and some type of government work, perhaps as a part of the diplomatic core, a lobbyist, or even an elected position. Either that or I was going to be a pop star, singing my way to fame. Two colleges and three majors later, I graduated with no real employment prospects. My combined music business and vocal performance degree from the esteemed New York University meant little as the horrific events of September 11,

2001, combined with the digital music revolution, gutted the music industry. At the urging of my former youth minister and dear friend, I applied for a coordinator of youth ministry role and the rest is history.

I had no idea what I was saying yes to upon beginning as a youth minister. Forget about the metaphor of being thrown into the deep end of the pool; I was dropped in the middle of the ocean during a typhoon. I not only quickly learned to swim, however, but somehow got to the metaphorical shore, bringing others with me. Now I can see that I was fueled by the fire of the Holy Spirit and that God was calling me to ministry. Upon closer examination, there were specific areas of giftedness at play: my drive to succeed, the ability to recognize and cultivate giftedness in others, a dedication to relational ministry, and my practice of surrounding myself with people more talented and knowledgeable than I. In addition, I developed a solid prayer practice of which my adult self is envious. It was not long until I found myself leading other endeavors at the parish: music ministry at the evening youth mass, the parish picnic, and a parish retreat to name just a few.

Since then, I have ministered for eighteen years, in five full-time positions covering three parishes in two different dioceses, handling everything from confirmation preparation to the RCIA and from youth band leader to communications director. Currently, I serve as the director of formation at a five-thousand-household parish in North Carolina. Together with the other seven members of our team, I oversee parish-wide formation programming and sacramental preparation for all ages. Just as it was not part of my plan to be a minister, I never imagined spearheading such a large endeavor in ministry would be in my future. For a long time my years of experience as a youth minister were enough to land a job, but once the opportunity for a director role opened up I knew I had to go back to school.

The past six years of graduate work have taught me that passion and experience are not enough to rise to the task of evangelizing and catechizing people in my community, as I cannot teach what I do not truly know. Being a woman in a leadership role in the church is challenging enough. My education has provided a certain legitimacy to the ministry I do. As I write this I have completed coursework for a certificate in church management from Villanova University and am one semester away from graduating from the University of Dallas with master's degrees in theological studies and catechetical ministry. Grad school has also revealed to me additional areas of interest and giftedness, connected me with a network of colleagues and mentors, and deepened my own faith. In addition, it has sparked much self-reflection as I wonder how I keep finding myself in the same position of being "put in charge" and yet still struggle to understand my role in the church. Here are some of the things I've discovered:

1. *Women in ministry are called to be simultaneously hospice workers and midwives.* A colleague shared this idea from her spiritual director with me after a particularly trying day. I am a hospice worker in that I must recognize when something is at the end of its life and help shepherd it to a dignified death. I acknowledge that the way things are is not necessarily the way things have to be or will always be. I am challenged to let old ways of clericalism, misogyny, legalism, and religious scrupulosity die. I am a midwife helping to birth something new, and I accompany and support during the pains of labor. I am called to be a prophet, on the lookout and aware that God is always doing something new, always breaking into our world in unexpected ways. I am tasked with pointing out the ways I see the Spirit moving in the church, and how lay people, especially women, are called to play a major part.

2. *If you need something, gather together a few women and ask them to dump out their handbags. Chances are you'll find what you need.*

The women I have encountered in ministry each have a "Mary Poppins" carpetbag filled with gifts, experience, and knowledge that are not necessarily apparent on a resume. I need to be unafraid to admit that something needed is not in my "bag" and invite other women to the table to share their gifts with the community and me. When I surround myself with people who are more gifted and talented in certain areas than I, they make me better and the community benefits from our collaboration. It does not take away from my own giftedness when others share theirs.

3. *The thing is not the thing.* This is a common saying in counseling, and it can easily be applied to about 80 percent of my personal interactions. Each individual I encounter brings his or her own baggage to a situation. I have to listen in a deep way to discover what those I lead are truly saying. If a parent is yelling at me about the registration deadline for a retreat, it is almost always an opportunity to minister. People are carrying more than what I can see at first glance. I have a chance to give grace at every turn and strive to be the type of person from whom people walk away feeling better and not worse.

4. *Do what you can with what you have; don't focus on what you're not doing and what you don't have.* Early in my career I would have terrible "program envy." I would read about another successful ministry endeavor or hear a speaker at a conference and feel really bad about myself, focusing on what I had not yet done or what my program did not look like. Time spent comparing myself to others is less time I have to cultivate my own giftedness and build my own programs. No person is perfect, and no program is perfect. I learned how to incorporate best practices and make them my own, but also to work with the gifts God has bestowed upon me.

5. *Saying yes to something means saying no to something else.* Many women, myself included, think they have to be Superwoman; they are driven to do everything and be everything to everyone.

For me, I know this stems from a desire to prove myself and show others that I can handle anything. This almost always sets me up for failure, because I simply *can't* do everything and be everything—it's impossible. Often saying yes to what I think I should be saying yes to takes time from worthwhile and fulfilling pursuits. It fractures my time and attention, and I end up not doing anything very well. I am learning to be intentional with my "yes" and to consider prayerfully what endeavors will best serve me, my family, and the community.

6. *People are not looking for perfection but for authenticity.* Walking alongside people of all ages in every stage of faith and sharing their joys and sorrows has been a sacred privilege and vocation. I have held parents as they buried children, visited hospitals in the wee hours of the morning, joyfully celebrated the marriages of youth ministry teens, made difficult phone calls about self-harm, ministered through community-wide scandal, navigated poor leadership, shared the hope that is ours in Christ Jesus, and encountered him in thousands of ways. I am always humbled that people let me share their journey for just a little while. Through many years of ministry I have realized that people want "Jesus with skin on him," as one of our friars loved to say. They are looking for a real person to walk alongside them, someone who knows what it is to be human, to suffer, to be imperfect. That I can be that person absolutely floors me. What a privileged role I play in the lives of others!

7. *Never underestimate the power of prayer and the sacraments.* Walking with those in the RCIA has given me a lot of time to reflect on the sacraments. Catholics don't believe that they are magic, but we do believe that something *actually happens* when we celebrate them. The same is true for prayer. Grace is poured out on us in ways we cannot even fathom. We are drawn more closely to Christ as we open ourselves to his saving power at work in our lives. Prayer changes me. Celebrating the sacraments

empowers me. These have an irreplaceable role in the life of any Christian, especially those of us who are leading others. When I give priority to these things, profound transformation happens.

8. *When you are moving up the ladder, look behind you to see whom you can give a hand up.* I stand on the shoulders of giants; the majority of them are women. I am thinking of our Blessed Mother, who fiercely proclaimed her Magnificat prayer and emboldens me to do the same. My biblical heroines, like the Samaritan woman who demands living water from Jesus, and the hemorrhaging woman in Mark's Gospel who dares to reach out and touch faith. Martha, who takes Jesus to task for allowing Lazarus to die, and Mary, who was the first person entrusted with the news of the resurrection. My own grandmother and mother, my high school youth minister, colleagues, professors, saints in heaven, and saints here on earth speaking truth and being hospice workers and midwives every day. These women, all leaders in their own ways, have blazed a path for me. Whenever I have the chance to do the same for another woman in ministry, I do so.

Several years back I received a letter from a young woman who was new to the area. She asked if she could take me to coffee to hear about the ministry that was happening in my diocese. It was a very busy and stressful time in my life, but I grudgingly agreed to meet her. I ended up hiring her at my parish, and it has been a great privilege to mentor her, watching her grow into one of the greatest pastoral ministers I have ever encountered.

And finally . . .

9. *Lead from wherever you are.* My drive to excel has led me to consider greater leadership roles, but I must never forget that I don't need to be in a named position to be a leader. At the core of Christian leadership is a servant's heart, and if I look to Jesus as an example, a nameplate on my door and formal title on a business card are not requirements. I am called to serve whomever I encounter, wherever I find them. And what does this service look

like? Going to the margins. Dining with the outcasts. Feeding the hungry. Healing the sick. Seeking the lost. In a parish setting it may mean getting youths the mental healthcare they need, finding scholarship money for summer camp, making a call to a homebound parishioner, giving others likely to be overlooked chances at ministry and leadership themselves, and above all, loving all those I encounter, meeting them wherever they are at. In the words of Madeleine L'Engle, "We draw people to Christ . . . by showing them a light that is so lovely that they want with all their hearts to know the source of it."[1]

---

[1] Madeleine L'Engle, *Walking on Water: Reflections on Faith and Art* (New York: Convergent Books, 2016), 172.

15

Laura Kaiser

*President and Chief Executive Officer, SSM Health,
St. Louis, Missouri*

With more than thirty years in healthcare, Laura S. Kaiser, FACHE, is a transformational leader and passionate advocate for the underserved. Driven by a deep sense of social justice, Ms. Kaiser has devoted her career to ensuring high-quality holistic care is affordable and accessible for all. As president/chief executive officer, Ms. Kaiser leads St. Louis, Missouri–based SSM Health. The Catholic not-for-profit health system serves communities across the Midwest through a robust and integrated health network that combines care delivery, a health plan, and a pharmacy benefit management company to create value and drive out unnecessary costs. Prior to joining SSM Health in May 2017, Ms. Kaiser held several senior leadership roles at Intermountain Healthcare and Ascension Health. She has also served on numerous boards, including the Catholic Health Association, Healthcare Leadership Council, Joint Commission Resources, Nuance Communications, Embold Health, and the Scottsdale Institute. Ms. Kaiser earned a bachelor of science from the University of Missouri, and a master of business administration and master of healthcare administration from Saint Louis University. She was named to *Modern Healthcare's* "100 Most Influential People in Healthcare" in 2018–20.

◇◇◇◇◇◇◇◇◇◇◇◇◇◇◇◇◇◇

Everyone remembers those kids in school who liked to bully their classmates, toy with defenseless creatures like insects or frogs, or even deface property in the neighborhood. Appalled at this behavior, I've felt a strong sense of justice for as long as I can remember. I'd like to say I've always spoken out for what I knew was right. The truth is there were times I wish I'd done more.

As leader of a large Catholic health system, my role includes making decisions every day that affect the lives of thousands of people, caring for more than forty thousand employees and providers, determining which communities to serve and which services to provide. My responsibility is to provide high-quality, accessible, and affordable healthcare for everyone regardless of ability to pay, with special attention to those who are physically, economically, and socially marginalized. Catholic social justice teaches us that all people are made in the image of God and so possess equal worth. Because of this essential dignity, all people have a right to all that is needed to allow them to live to full potential as intended by God. Additionally, leading a health ministry with Franciscan roots, our calling includes preservation of the earth, doing our part to help protect wildlife and precious, finite resources. Catholic healthcare is a vital ministry of the church, and I take it seriously.

Growing up in the Midwest, the foundation of faith, community, and hard work from a very early age was emphasized. My family was active in our local church and community, and volunteering in a variety of activities was routine. With the support and encouragement of my parents, along with many supportive mentors and sponsors through the years, I pursued my education, work experience, and found my calling in healthcare administration.

My first internship in health administration was at a Catholic hospital. There I found the values, strong sense of community, service to others, focus on social justice, and needs that aligned well with my personal values. Being able to bring my whole self to work each day felt like a gift. It still does.

Over the years, the opportunity to grow and contribute to this rich health ministry has manifested in countless ways. I've spent many hours with women religious just soaking up their wisdom, kindness, and perspectives, watching them lead and listening to their advice on how to continue courageously, persevere, and build character and community. Along the way, investments in ongoing formation have been made—including daily prayer, a two-year leadership formation program, learning new words like *eschatological,* working with a spiritual director, participating in retreats, and a pilgrimage to Assisi and Rome, Italy.

As part of health ministry work, volunteering at a local soup kitchen periodically occurs, and I've noticed that people appear to have varying levels of comfort around others who may be on a difficult path or life journey. At times it can be seemingly hard to find common ground. While every volunteer heartily pitches in to cook, prepare, serve, clear tables, and wash dishes, rare is the volunteer who chooses to sit with the clients, just spending time in fellowship. Over the years one of my colleagues consistently did this—he was present, seeing the face of God in each person, fostering a sense of connection and of being seen, heard, and loved. Without saying a word he taught me that serving is important and so is being fully present to really connect with the person you're serving. I've never forgotten that lesson.

There are countless frameworks leaders can utilize to hone skills, and I've found the seven gifts of the Holy Spirit is one that speaks to me. The seven gifts are wisdom, understanding, counsel, fortitude, knowledge, fear of the Lord, and piety. Aspiring to all of these, I am clearly a work in process. My focus is principally to deepen wisdom, fortitude, and piety. Wisdom includes the ability to listen, to exercise good judgment, and to seek and uphold truth and justice. Fortitude represents resiliency, courage, and patience to always do what is right. Finally, piety is about servant leadership, devotion to God, and putting others' needs above your own.

In Catholicism, we are taught that a person who receives these gifts of the Holy Spirit in the sacrament of confirmation must put them to good use. In Luke 12:48, Jesus said, "To whom much is given, much will be required." Some assume that only wealthy or powerful people have been given much, but the truth is we have all been given much. It's up to each of us to be good stewards of our individual blessings of talents, knowledge, wisdom, and resources.

Finally, having served as a leader for many years, I often receive requests for career advice. First, I ask what the person cares about to help point toward an area that speaks to the person's passion. Personally, it's about making a difference, being a good steward, and leaving things better for the people served by the health ministry and for the next generation of leaders. Just as Catholic social justice points out, that includes helping others reach their potential, encouraging and actively assisting them on their career paths and life journeys. It is thrilling to witness and foster people's growth. It is also completely aligned with driving organizational performance to reach the potential of the organization.

Second, I encourage those seeking career advice to devote time to understand deeply the unique gifts and talents they may have been blessed with and are expected to use. Knowing one's strengths is not prideful—it's just as important as understanding blind spots and areas in which one needs to grow. In my current role it is about being visionary—looking to the future; ensuring our board, leadership, and team members are aligned; driving the health ministry forward in pursuit of fulfilling our mission of providing exceptional healthcare revealing the presence of God and representing SSM Health well in every setting. I am expected to bring my best self and everything I have to this calling—and given the amount of change and transformation needed in our industry, it requires my all.

Third, self-care is an essential ingredient in leadership. When preparing for an in-flight emergency, we're directed to put on our own oxygen mask before we help someone else—and it's true not just on airplanes but in life. People count on leaders to be prepared, focused, and solid. Leaders cannot do their best unless they are taking care of spiritual, emotional, mental, and physical needs. For me, that principally translates into daily prayer, fitness, healthy eating, and time that isn't scheduled and is "off the grid." I enjoy spending time with family and friends, reading, running, cycling, and generally being active, particularly after a stressful day. So, my advice for everyone, particularly women, is to find ways to nourish your body and soul each day. It's one of the most unselfish things you can do for those you care about.

In sum, I return to where this story began. At my core is a deep sense of justice that consistently guides my choices, energy, and work. I've found that Catholic health ministry is a place that seeks social justice through healthcare within the walls of the hospital and in the communities that health systems like SSM Health serve. I've also found it does this best when we are in community with one another. If we are still and listen for God's voice, we can best serve as the instruments to implement God's plan to honor and provide dignity for every person and living creature in the work we are called to do. As one leader in Catholic healthcare, it is a blessing to be one of those instruments.

16

Sister Carol Keehan, DC

(Retired) President and Chief Executive Officer, Catholic Health Association, Washington, DC

Sister Carol Keehan leads the Health Task Force of the Vatican COVID-19 Commission, established by Pope Francis in March 2020 to respond to the global devastation caused by the pandemic. She is the former president and CEO of the Catholic Health Association of the United States and was responsible for all the Catholic Health Association's operations in the St. Louis and Washington, DC, offices. Sister Carol has been president and CEO of hospitals for over eighteen years. She held influential roles in the governance of healthcare, insurance, and educational organizations. She was elected to the National Academy of Medicine and appointed to the International Federation of Catholic Health Care Associations of the Pontifical Council for Pastoral Health Care, Catholic Relief Services board, and more. A member of several health, labor, and domestic policy committees of the United States Conference of Catholic Bishops, she also serves on the finance committee of the Archdiocese of Washington, DC. Sister Carol earned a master of science in business administration from the University of South Carolina, a bachelor of science degree in nursing, and has been awarded eleven honorary doctoral degrees.

◇◇◇◇◇◇◇◇◇◇◇◇◇◇◇◇

My most public leadership role was as president and CEO of the Catholic Health Association of United States (CHA). CHA has over 635 hospitals and 1,400 other healthcare facilities in its membership. My prior leadership roles as hospital president, vice president for nursing, supervisor of a children's hospital, staff nurse, and nurse aide significantly influenced my leadership style and decisions in my CHA role. Living daily with the challenges of providing quality care to diverse patients in multiple roles and settings gave me a clear view of the contributions and struggles of many healthcare positions in direct care and support staff. For example, the potential of the most talented surgeon is lost if the right equipment is not at hand, or if it has not been properly sterilized, or if the electricity goes out in a storm and the emergency generator does not come on.

Living up close for many years with patients and families impacted by many illnesses was a grace but often a painful education. This is especially true when economics is the barrier, and watching that become more of a barrier in each decade of my career was especially painful. As healthcare had more and better options for prevention and cures, they became available to fewer and fewer families. The economic impact on many to get basic care drove out many other dreams such as housing, education, and vacations as they coped with the ever-increasing cost of basic healthcare.

Except for choosing to study nursing and my last job with CHA, none of the positions I held were ever my choice, and some were positions I prayed to be spared. I came to love every one of them, and each had a profound impact on me. All challenged me to learn new skills and gave me opportunities I would have never dreamed I would have. For instance, taking on a very troubled nursing department led to a wonderful experience of the transformation of it and a thirty-year avocation of healthcare education for Japanese health professionals. These experiences have left me with the conviction that being open to things you never thought possible and hoped would never happen can be extraordinarily enriching and prepare one for even better opportunities and experiences. I have tried to share this with other young people so they don't miss opportunities that could really enrich their lives.

The other side of this coin is that these experiences often bring one face to face with deficits that must be addressed if one is to be as successful as one aspires to be. For me, it became clear that my goals of quality care for all, especially the most vulnerable, and just treatment of staff were not going to be achieved by me without a major new skill set: financial skills. I have said to many people that I had great ideas that were easily shot down when I could not relate to their impact on Medicare reimbursement, insurance contracts, physician contracts, and other financial issues. It meant taking undergraduate prerequisites like accounting and then getting a master's in healthcare finances. Knowing what else you need and going after it is one thing I have worked diligently to encourage young professionals to do.

The other deficit was advocacy/political skills. The market and financial issues play a controlling role in healthcare but definitely not the only role. Our federal, state, and local governments are major controlling factors. They can be major forces for good or genuine roadblocks. Unfortunately, given the convoluted health financing system that has evolved in the United States, officials often do not even understand the impact of their decisions.

Sadly, those most negatively affected by legislation and regulations are often least able to advocate effectively for themselves. They rarely have a voice at the table. Having the advantage of being part of a major healthcare provider gives one the potential to be at the table. Using this advantage well means understanding the system, how to use it, choosing to use it for the right things, and being willing to continue to find effective ways to help the most vulnerable. This is a skill set most health professionals do not acquire in school. However, there are ways to learn it, and the voice of those who see up close how the system fails the most vulnerable should be at the table.

I was fortunate to be a young professional supervising a children's hospital in Florida committed to caring for every child, not just the insured. Florida politics at the state and local level is an art form for sure. I was also the beneficiary of the example of very smart and powerful but humble lay men. Their support provided me with guidance that I used then and many times later, even as I helped navigate the challenges of getting enough votes to pass the ACA. I could never thank them enough, and if I have been successful in any advocacy or political efforts, they deserve the credit.

17

Ann Murphy Manion

Founder and President, Women's Care Center,
South Bend, Indiana

Since 1988, Ann Manion has served as president and CEO of Women's Care Center on a volunteer basis. The center is the nation's largest, most successful pregnancy-resource center, serving more women in more locations than any other. She was also a founding board member of Hannah's House, a maternity home for pregnant women, jointly founded by St. Joseph Hospital of Mishawaka and Women's Care Center in 1993. During her tenure as president, Women's Care Center has grown from one small center in South Bend, Indiana, to thirty-three centers in twelve states, serving four hundred women every day. The center is funded almost entirely through private donations. The center was also recently awarded the Evangelium Vitae Award from the University of Notre Dame DeNicola Center for Ethics and Culture, the first time a pregnancy center has received this national award. Ann graduated magna cum laude from the University of Notre Dame in 1977 with a bachelor's degree in business administration. She was a senior manager with Price Waterhouse from 1977 to 1988. Ann is married to Daniel Manion, a judge on the 7th Circuit Court of Appeals. They have four children—Mary, Katherine, Patrick, and Michael.

◇◇◇◇◇◇◇◇◇◇◇◇◇◇◇◇◇◇

Looking back, I see so clearly the hand of God in my life. I didn't have a grand plan. But God did. I was born into a large Catholic family. My dad was a law professor at the University of Notre Dame. My mom was a stay-at-home mom to nine children; all but two of us were boys. I always assumed growing up that I would follow in her footsteps. When it came time for college, the University of Notre Dame was just starting to accept women. And with free tuition for faculty kids, this was a natural for me. Initially, I thought I might go to college to become a teacher. But at the time, there was a glut of teachers. And many of the women I worked summers with on the teller line at the local bank were out-of-work teachers.

I didn't want to invest in all that schooling to end up back on the teller line. So, at the advice of my dad, I pivoted into a practical major—accounting! Dad's theory was that accounting was a lot like law but required fewer years of schooling, which was appealing. Surprisingly, I found out that I was good at accounting. After graduation, I accepted a job with Price Waterhouse. The work was interesting. I enjoyed the people and initially I enjoyed the travel. Year after year I received promotions and moved up the line in the public accounting world. I got married and wanted children. But the children didn't come on my timeline. After nine years in public accounting, I decided to leave and gave the firm a year's notice. I didn't know what I was going to do next. But I knew I wanted children, and the travel and stress of this job (although I loved it!) didn't seem to be compatible with that goal. The one-year notice gave Price Waterhouse time to transition my clients and seemed like a gracious way to end things. It was not until I decided to leave that I finally became pregnant with my first baby, Mary. And just a few weeks after I walked out the door of Price Waterhouse, she was born. It seemed the perfect time to give stay-at-home mothering a try. But as God would have it, there was another plan.

Over the years I had become involved with a small Catholic pregnancy center in South Bend, Women's Care Center. The center was founded in 1984 by Catholic theologian and former University of Notre Dame professor Dr. Janet E. Smith. It was my only sister, Mary, who introduced me to this work. Mary was on the founding board of the center and recruited me. She insisted that the center needed an accountant, and I was it. Just as I was settling into being the mother of a newborn, founder Janet Smith decided to leave the community, and Women's Care Center suddenly needed a new leader. Janet took me out for pizza and insisted that I was perfect for the job. If you know Janet, you know she is difficult to say no to. At first, I was primarily in a board leadership role and less involved in the day to day. But as we grew, I found that my business skills were needed. And I grew to love and greatly appreciate the mission.

Today, I believe that I found my vocation with Women's Care Center in addition to my family. As my family grew, Women's Care Center grew as well. I now have four children, ages twenty-two to thirty-two. And one small pregnancy center in Indiana has become thirty-three centers in twelve states. Today, Women's Care Center serves more women and saves more babies than any pregnancy center in the nation, with over sixteen thousand babies born to our moms last year alone. Today, this Catholic mission is a pro-life ministry run like a business and highly replicable. The hardest decision for me was in 1990 when we decided to expand from one center to two. Our tiny little blue house that was the original Women's Care Center was overflowing! My first thought was to open a second center just down the block. But through an amazing set of "coincidences," we were saved from what would have been a very poor decision. The nearby center fell through. And local Bishop John D'Arcy brokered a deal to get us free space at an office building owned by the Catholic hospital in Mishawaka. An incredible thing happened! By locating six miles away, instead of just down the block, we found a whole new population of women in need of care. This started the explosive growth that has continued to this day.

And there have been so many miracles every step of the way. The Catholic hospital in Mishawaka had a unique idea for a fundraiser (a house raffle) and wanted a sympathetic charity to co-sponsor it. The proceeds from this annual house raffle were initially more than our entire budget. Thus, the birth of centers number three and four. Crazy idea after crazy idea came our way through the grace of God. We just had to say yes. A small center in an adjoining county wanted to become a Women's Care Center. Yes. A businessman in Fort Wayne had a house he wanted to donate for a new Women's Care Center there. Yes. A major benefactor family to the University of Notre Dame wanted a center in their hometown of Columbus, Ohio. A volunteer from our Fort Wayne center moved to Peoria, Illinois, and wanted to open a center there. A young nurse at one of our centers moved to Nebraska with her family and wanted to open a center there. Opportunity after opportunity came our way, and so often we were able to witness the direct hand of God in our work.

In Milwaukee, we ran afoul of the zoning board due to the interference of a local alderman who didn't like our Catholic mission. We had high-level support from Father John Jenkins at the University of Notre Dame. Bishop D'Arcy also recruited Cardinal Dolan and Archbishop Listecki to appeal on our behalf. But the situation seemed hopeless. That is, until one hour after the completion of a nine-day Novena to St. Joseph . . . when astonishingly, the city gave in. I am not, nor have I ever been, involved in direct client care, but our counselors report much the same thing. Babies who should not be here today, but for miracles. The GPS takes a woman to our center instead of the abortion clinic. The five-week-old baby already has a beating heart. A woman turns her life around with just a little bit of confidence. And the donors who create miracles. In the early days I remember a $10,000 gift that arrived at a time when we otherwise couldn't meet payroll. And the eighty-year-old woman who recruited all her friends to help open a center in Fort Pierce, Florida. And, of course, the many, many people who showed up with diapers and donations to help Women's Care Center weather the storm and stay open during the COVID-19 crisis.

The miracles happened, and the opportunities presented themselves. And I've learned a lot of important lessons along the way. I've learned that many of the same successful principles that work in business also work in the not-for-profit Catholic ministry world. I've learned to be open to new opportunities always, although it's important to check motives along the way and make sure what we say yes to is guided by our mission. After a decision is made and a course of action is chosen, I've learned always to project more confidence than I feel. As my mother-in-law used to say, "The world steps aside for the woman who knows where she is going." Finally, it takes a great team. I have also learned to "get the right people on the bus" and empower them.

And what has made this so fun for me is that it has become a family affair. My kids were raised at the Women's Care Center. And despite mishaps like my daughters learning about sex at a young age by reading our client pamphlets, all are strong in their Catholic faith and share a deep commitment to this mission. All my children worked for Women's Care Center at one time or another. Mary was a counselor in Columbus, Ohio. Patrick serves as our business manager/human resources lead. Mikey, my youngest (a college student), has worked security, childcare, and whatever else needs to be done. And today my daughter Katherine serves as our national outreach director. A Purdue MBA, Katherine has also decided to dedicate her life to this mission that I love.

18

Sister Donna Markham, OP

President, Catholic Charities USA, Washington, DC

Sr. Donna, president of Catholic Charities USA, is the first woman to hold this position in the organization's over one-hundred-year history. An Adrian Dominican Sister with a doctorate in clinical psychology, Sr. Donna has served in behavioral healthcare leadership positions in Canada and the United States. She is an internationally recognized author and speaker in areas of transformational leadership, organizational change management, and the effective treatment of the mentally ill. Sr. Donna received her doctorate from the University of Detroit and has been involved in executive leadership development, organizational transformation, and clinical practice throughout her professional career. Before coming to Catholic Charities USA, she served as president of the Behavioral Health Institute at Mercy Health, where she led the transformation of the delivery of behavioral health services across the seven geographic regions of the health system. She has served as prioress of the Adrian Dominican Congregation and as president of the Leadership Conference of Women Religious. Donna is a fellow in the American Academy of Clinical Psychologists. In addition to executive management and clinical work, Sr. Donna is engaged in global peace initiatives directed toward building bridges of understanding and collaboration across conflict zones.

◇◇◇◇◇◇◇◇◇◇◇◇◇◇◇

Throughout my life as a Dominican Sister and a clinical psychologist, I have served in a number of significant leadership roles, mostly at the executive level. Within what we commonly understand to be Catholic Church–related institutions, I have served as a member of the general council of the Adrian Dominican Sisters and later as prioress of the congregation. During my time in leadership of the Adrian Dominicans, I was elected president of the Leadership Conference of Women Religious. Beyond leadership in religious life, I also served as the executive director of the Dominican Consultation Center in Detroit, Michigan; as a professor of psychology at St. John Provincial Seminary in Michigan; as president of the Southdown Institute in Ontario, Canada; as president of the Behavioral Health Institute of Mercy Health in Ohio; and as president and CEO of Catholic Charities USA. In three of these institutions I was the first woman to hold the position.

While I seldom thought about that fact, it is apparent in hindsight that I was frequently confronted in the hiring process with interview questions that focused on my ability to assume a leadership role that had previously been held by a man, often by a member of the clergy. For example, I recall being asked about my age (then young), my appearance, and my gender, and how I could ever manage to teach and keep "classroom discipline" with seminarians who were only a few years younger than I. I also recall a male search committee member for one institution commenting on my appearance, clothing, and capacity to engage successfully with members of the hierarchy. With some amusement now, I recall an interchange with him that went something like this: "Well, that's a pretty classy haircut, a fancy silk shirt, and nice cufflinks *for a nun*," to which I immediately responded, "Cut my own hair, polyester shirt, my dad's cufflinks!" I realized immediately that no interviewer would make comments like that to a male candidate. These examples, admittedly, occurred in the 1980s and 1990s. Interestingly, once in the positions, I never experienced my gender lessening my credibility or diminishing my ability to lead effectively.

I credit a number of people with helping me grow into a strong, competent woman. Of course, my parents were the earliest formative influence on my life. As the oldest of five siblings, I was trusted at an early age to be responsible. It is fair to say that I was a serious child, often timid and quietly studious. My parents recognized that I had a decent mind and continually encouraged me not to be afraid to use it. While my parents were highly educated and intelligent, my mother was wickedly bright and quite strong. She was a true role model for being a strong, compassionate woman.

Throughout the course of my education I was exposed to incredible academic leaders and teachers, many of whom were women, and not the least of whom were the Adrian Dominican Sisters. I experienced them as intelligent, fun, holy, and committed women dedicated to pursuing what was true and good. They grounded my academic life in the practice of using my brain to help make a difference.

During the formative years of secondary school and undergraduate studies at the University of Toronto, I was immersed in the cultural ethos of the civil rights movement, the antiwar movement, and the women's movement. The folk music of Joan Baez; Peter, Paul, and Mary; Pete Seeger; Bob Dylan; and Woody Guthrie—to name a few—seeped into my soul and woke me up emotionally to the consequences of evil, violence, and discrimination. Freedom songs and war-protest ballads made up much of the music of those times. Along with the music, the growing pull of the documents of Vatican II and wonderfully provocative theology professors all had some part to play in causing me to consider how I might make some difference in an unsettled world. My choices narrowed to joining the Peace Corps or joining the Adrian Dominicans. The Dominicans won that one.

After three years of teaching in elementary and secondary school, the Dominicans invited me to apply for doctoral studies in clinical psychology. My training at the University of Detroit was grounded in classical psychodynamic theory and practice. Upon finishing my doctorate, I worked in the psychiatric department of a large Jewish teaching hospital. There I was blessed to have an extraordinary woman psychologist, who served as chief of the service, as my mentor. She was certainly a role model for exercising leadership in a primarily male-dominated clinical environment.

I was always particularly intrigued by how that classical theoretical foundation could be applied to group psychotherapy and, later, to large and small group dynamics in the workplace and across organizations. Much of that thinking is included in the book I wrote nearly twenty years ago, *Spiritlinking Leadership: Working through Resistance to Organizational Change.* Particularly formative was my immersion in attachment theory and how those insights applied to becoming a good leader. To this day I would acknowledge that theoretical grounding operates as a kind of leitmotif, acting as a quiet backdrop throughout my ministry as a leader.

Trained initially in fine art and philosophy and later in clinical psychology, I had absolutely no academic training in business, management, finance, accounting, or investing. I searched out great mentors in those areas of expertise who served as my teachers and consultants throughout my professional life.

My religious life has followed no "career path." My work as a psychologist was regularly interrupted by humbling calls to serve in leadership in the Adrian Dominican Congregation and in the Leadership Conference of Women Religious. Each time, upon completion of my term of office, I returned to my clinical work, usually assuming some role in executive leadership. I have realized that being a leader within my religious congregation prepared me well for a highly participative, team-based way of leading in other organizational positions. Religious leadership following Vatican II moved drastically away from any tinge of a hieratic exercise of authority. Because I was often the first woman to hold a particular organizational leadership position, staff members—and sometimes board members—were often perplexed by how I operated. Perplexed as they were, I believe they came to value a different leadership style. I would have to say that each position I have held over the years has been a joy. I have somehow never experienced having the team or the staff turning on me. On the contrary, I have felt privileged to serve with them and have felt stretched by their dedication and goodness. That may sound pollyannaish, but it is my experience. This is certainly not to say that I have escaped the challenges of having to deal with an irascible character or two from time to time!

I share this simply to say that I am uncomfortable with top-down leadership models in this day and age, whether in the corporate world or the church sector. Admittedly, I have not often had to deal with directly reporting to a male corporate leader or member of the clergy because I have held executive leadership positions more often. My life journey has taken me to other places. For that reason, I don't carry many residual memories from bad experiences with male superiors. The times when my "bosses" were lay men or clergy, I found most of them to be wonderful leaders.

If nothing else, this brief snapshot of my growth as a leader attests to the fact that God, indeed, works in strange ways!

19

Bernarda "Berni" Neal

*Board Member and Former Board Chair, Catholic
Leadership Institute, Orange County, California*

After a professional career in advertising, Berni Neal now dedicates
her time to Catholic evangelization and philanthropy. Neal currently
serves on the governing boards of Catholic Leadership Institute, Endow, EWTN, Legatus, Live Action, Magnificat Foundation, and Thomas
Aquinas College. Neal's committee work includes Given, WorldPriest,
Woodson Center–Free Speech/Civil Rights Coalition, and the Committee to Eradicate Human Trafficking. Together with her husband,
Rob, she is a member of the Legatus Orange Coast Chapter and the
Papal Foundation. They reside in Newport Beach, California. They have
two adult children and one grandchild.

Sometime in 1968, the 1943 movie *The Song of Bernadette* was
going to air on TV. My ritual scan of the Sunday TV weekly
guide had revealed this wonderful movie title with my name on
it! I was named after St. Bernadette. I circled it twice. My parents
were very forgiving about my marking up the *TV Guide* this
way week after week. My parents are both immigrants. Spanish is their first language. Television provided a connection to

Spanish-language programming, limited as it was, and it also gave them insight to the American culture and the ability to refine their English-language skills and accents. They were not avid TV watchers, but they had a small black-and-white TV perched on their bedroom dresser. I asked my parents for permission to watch the movie in their room because I wanted to watch it without my little brother and sister interrupting or even my parents bothering me. I wanted a private viewing of this curious movie with MY saint's name on it. It was a sublime night. Vivid affirmation that heaven exists. I knew it all along because my prayers were going somewhere, but this was a huge revelation, on TV no less.

I loved church. I loved getting ready (my mom always chose from my nice clothes). I loved my white veil in the plastic pouch with bobby pins tucked inside. I loved my mom's long black veil and the beautiful box that held her rosary. I loved the weekly envelope with the date stamped outside. I loved lying on the kneelers during mass and looking at people's shoes. But St. Bernadette! She SAW Our Lady. She was so brave, so humble, so convicted . . . not much older than me. She also loved Our Lady, in spite of everything that the adults were doing to her. She loved Our Lady . . . and so began my awareness of grace, of the bridge between heaven and earth, of the ability to fight on behalf of heaven here on earth.

Along the way I have had moments when I needed the child-like understanding that courage would be forthcoming. I just had to say yes. I would venture to say that I have those moments every day!

20

Karen Dolan Rauenhorst

Vice-Chair, Catholic Relief Services Foundation,
Minneapolis, Minnesota

Karen Dolan Rauenhorst is a 1975 graduate of Creighton University School of Nursing. She earned a master's degree in public health with an emphasis in maternal and child health in 1987 from the University of Minnesota. For over fifteen years she worked in various nursing leadership roles in healthcare. For the past twenty-five years she has spent a significant amount of time on nonprofit boards, including Catholic Charities and Catholic Relief Services, serving those in poverty and on the margins of society. Her philanthropy work has included serving on the boards of Better Way Foundation, Aim Higher Foundation, CRS Foundation, Catholic Community Foundation (CCF), Foundation and Donors Interested in Catholic Activities, and the Mark and Karen Rauenhorst Foundation. She provided her insights on leadership with the local church as a trustee of Holy Name of Jesus Parish for eleven years and trustee at the Archdiocese of St. Paul and Minneapolis for ten years. Mrs. Rauenhorst received an honorary doctor of law degree from the University of Notre Dame, an Alumni Achievement Citation award from Creighton University, a Legacy of Faith award from CCF, and an honorary doctor of humane letters from St. Catherine University.

◇◇◇◇◇◇◇◇◇◇◇◇◇◇◇◇

Over the past forty years the major leadership roles I have assumed in Catholic organizations have been on governing boards
and committees of the organizations with which I volunteered.
These leadership roles include social service agencies and elementary, high school, and higher educational institutions. I also
currently serve on the National Catholic Education Association
(NCEA) board. I was one of the first three women invited onto
the board of Catholic Relief Services, the international relief
organization. I have worked with clerics as a parish trustee and
corporate trustee at the Archdiocese of St. Paul and Minneapolis. I was the Catholic Community Foundation vice-chair in its
formative years and currently chair the Governance Committee
for Foundation and Donors Interested in Catholic Activities,
FADICA. I continue to be active with the Aim Higher Foundation, a scholarship-granting foundation of which I was the
founding chair.

    As I reflect on how and why I spent most of my volunteer-
ing in Catholic institutions, I recognize the importance of my
education, my curiosity, and the example my parents set to help
create this path on which I have been. My parents served their
community in their own unique way. My father, a physician,
never denied care to anyone who came to his office. Most of
the patients' hardships were because of financial challenges, and
many times they paid their bills with food from their gardens or
some homemade goodies. We could always count on some extra
special treats around Christmas time! My dad never judged and
just mentioned some of his patients were down on their luck and
needed a little extra help. My mother often consoled her friends
and family members by being present at their time of need with
a basket full of food and her specialty, homemade cakes. What
my parents did to help others, such as my dad's patients, family,
or friends, was always a part of everyday life for me growing up
in Iowa. It was our family culture.

I experienced a significant impact on my career and curiosity with Native Americans in the summer of 1971. Three of my best friends and I had just graduated from high school and were going to volunteer with the Franciscan Sisters from Dubuque, Iowa. We planned to live together in a major urban city in the Midwest or South and work with kids in these communities for six weeks. We all thought this was a great way to spend the summer and do some volunteer service work before going to college. When the assignments came, one friend went to Sioux City, Iowa; one to Dubuque, Iowa; and, to my surprise, I was assigned to the Pine Ridge Reservation in South Dakota. The impact of working with the sisters and teaching bible school for six weeks in different villages on the reservation that summer created an interest and curiosity that remain present in me today. I thank God for this opportunity, even though I could not share it with my friends.

My educational journey began when I attended a Catholic elementary and high school, Columbus, in Waterloo, Iowa. For college, I attended Creighton University, a Jesuit institution. The Jesuit education had a profound impact on me, and I have tried to make the Jesuit core values part of who I am:

- *Unity of heart, mind, and soul:* A kind heart, an open mind, and a strong purpose work together as a personal and communal triumvirate. All three are essential to becoming one's strongest self and creating community.
- *Women and men for others:* Through selfless action, we can all achieve more. When we all step forward with the best versions of ourselves, we invite and enable others to do the same.
- *Forming and educating agents of change:* Identifying passions and honing skills are the first steps toward making a meaningful, lasting difference. It is also important to embrace learning and leading as two sides of the same transformative coin.

These values were a part of the nursing program at Creighton. I received a bachelor of science in nursing in 1975. After working in a hospital clinical area, mainly in supervision for ten years, I completed a master's in public health, focusing on maternal–child health in 1989. In the late 1980s I left the healthcare workforce and started volunteering for Catholic Charities of St. Paul and Minneapolis, Women and Children's Division. I joined the Catholic Charities board in 1989, my first board experience and first Catholic organization in which I assumed a significant leadership role. I was able to leverage my previous leadership skills from working in a hospital setting and managing several large departments. This experience helped me, alongside others, transform the board structure and make a significant change in board and management leadership practices at Catholic Charities.

Over the next forty years I either was the chairperson or vice-chair of six different Catholic organizations' boards. I was on five other Catholic boards, where I chaired the governance or strategic-planning process. Over the same time I served on eight other boards that involved healthcare organizations and foundations. Several leadership skills that I learned early in my healthcare career and employed in all my board work are the following:

- *Respect* all the individuals with whom you work and realize their voices and insights have something to offer in every conversation. Often the person working at the front desk of these organizations has remarkable insights. As I was heading into a meeting with the CEO at Catholic Chari-ties, the front-desk manager would share who had been in the office, what he had for lunch, and most important, what his mood was. This insight set me up for a successful meeting in dealing with difficult conversations with the older, stubborn monsignor.

- *Passion* for the work I do is the driving force that keeps me motivated. It is so important to know that you and your coworkers and volunteers are committed to your organization's mission and values. For example, I know that children with a diverse background who receive a Catholic education will have greater opportunities in their future. This passion for giving more children the chance to receive a Catholic education is social justice action.

- *Collaboration* with your coworkers and partners leads to excellent outcomes. I learned that when you create collaboration and networks with other Catholic organizations, you tend to expand your horizon and find new ways of accomplishing your mission for the organization. One example is with the American Indian Catholic Schools Network, a part of Notre Dame's Alliance for Catholic Education program. This group of now eight Catholic Native American schools from all different Native nations has collaborated for almost three years on best practices in education for faculty and students. The members have found that they have more issues and opportunities in common than they ever thought. By creating this network and collaborating, all the Catholic school leaders, children, and families have been positively affected by the schools' improvements.

I found that there were skill sets I had to learn for the roles that I served on different boards. The most important new knowledge that I needed to understand was business acumen, such as interpreting financial statements, understanding investment reports, and doing long-term financial projections for organizations. Another area where I had to expand my knowledge was understanding the role of canon law in relation to many Catholic entities. Canon law for some Catholic organizations is as critical to understanding an organization as civil legal issues. For example, in determining the viability of a parish and its future, many canon law issues need to be addressed in concert with all the financial and personnel matters. The way I stayed current on critical issues facing the institution was constantly

engaging with the organization's management-leadership team.
I also relied on expert board members who understood these
issues. I would seek their knowledge and insight into the topics
pertinent to board discussions ahead of time. I also sought inde-
pendent resources and researched business issues and the impact
of canon law in specific areas of interest.

What has helped guide and encourage me to stay engaged and
participate in so many Catholic organizations as a lay woman are
the principles of Catholic social teaching that I learned early on
at Catholic Charities. These guiding principles come from the
Office of Social Justice in Minnesota:

- Human dignity
- Community and the common good
- Rights and responsibilities
- Options for the poor and vulnerable
- Participation
- Dignity of work and rights of workers
- Stewardship of creation
- Solidarity
- Promotion of peace

I have had many interesting experiences and educational opportunities throughout my fifty-plus years in Catholic leadership.
These different experiences greatly influenced my work as a lay
woman in the Catholic Church. I was able to do this work with
the support of my husband and children. I also have a strong
faith guided by the church's moral teaching and a spiritual life
that nourishes me daily. My Catholic faith has been a significant
part of making this journey joyful in good times and in difficult
and challenging times. Women leaders need to stay vigilant and
engaged in all the work of the Catholic Church, just as Mary did.

21

Annemarie Reilly

Chief of Staff and Executive Vice President of Strategy, Technology, and Communications, Catholic Relief Services, Baltimore, Maryland

At CRS, Annemarie Reilly serves alongside her over seven thousand colleagues worldwide who deliver programs and services that reach over 150 million people annually. She is committed to the agency's mission to provide opportunities for all people to live to their full God-given human potential in more just, equitable, and peaceful societies where humankind prospers in harmony with our natural environment. She draws inspiration for this work from the gospel of Jesus Christ as well as from the extraordinary people—program participants, partners, colleagues, church workers and leaders, donors, supporters—she has been privileged to meet and learn from around the world. In three decades with CRS Annemarie has served in El Salvador, Haiti, Burundi, Liberia, Kenya, South Africa, and Zambia. Her field experience includes roles as country representative, regional director, and head of CRS's Global Emergency Response team. Annemarie holds bachelor of arts degrees in government and French from the University of Notre Dame and a master's in international affairs from the Columbia University School of International and Public Affairs, specializing in economic and political development and Latin American studies.

<><><><><><><><><><><>

St. Oscar Romero of El Salvador said:

> Each one of you has to be God's microphone. Each one
> of you has to be a messenger, a prophet. The Church will
> always exist as long as there is someone who has been
> baptized. . . . Where is your baptism? You are baptized in
> your professions, in the fields of workers, in the market.
> Wherever there is someone who has been baptized, that is
> where the Church is. There is a prophet there. Let us not
> hide the talent that God gave us on the day of our baptism
> and let us truly live the beauty and responsibility of being
> a prophetic people.[1]

I currently serve as chief of staff and executive vice president
of strategy, technology, and communications at CRS, the international humanitarian arm of the US Catholic community. CRS's
work is inspired by a vision rooted in Catholic teaching for a
world where all people can live to their full potential. The gap
between this vision and the world as we know it is enormous.
Three decades of tremendous progress in the areas of health,
education, and income are now in a reversing trend, exacerbated
by a pandemic, violent conflicts, and abuse of the natural environment God has given us. Working to close the gap can seem
a fool's errand in today's world. But isn't this precisely the work
to which the church calls all of the faithful? Leadership from
this perspective is in all of us if the question is how we cultivate
our talents and direct them toward being the prophetic people
St. Romero calls us to be.

One of eight siblings, I fed off the energy and creativity of
a boisterous household to cultivate my talents. The first of two

---

[1] "Man as God's Microphone: 11 Quotes to Celebrate the Life and Voice
of Oscar Romero," Central America, Voices for Justice, Ignatian Solidarity
Network, August 13, 2014.

girls, I grew up in the late 1960s through the mid 1980s, determined to compete on equal footing with the boys. And in my household that meant lots of sports, including being one of the first girls in my town to play Little League Baseball. It also meant that I grew up feeling a bit of the underdog with something to prove—the girl who wanted to play against the boys. I also grew up encouraged by my father to step up and to stick my neck out. I am an introvert by nature, so suffice it to say I wasn't always a willing participant in challenging norms. In hindsight, my father's pushing me out of my comfort zone provided initial life lessons in leadership that have stayed with me throughout my life.

My parents struggled to meet the growing needs of a large family on a modest income. My mother was devoted to raising her children, consistently voicing an unfailing faith-filled belief in the power of love. I look back and wonder at what seemed to be my mother's infinite patience and my father's ability to keep all of us active in sports, music, and art lessons—anything that had us moving, being creative, and developing our talents. We were given gifts, and he believed we had a responsibility to explore and cultivate them.

My desire to apply my talents to the church's humanitarian and development work emerged from a fusing together of my faith and professional interests while a student at the University of Notre Dame. While my Catholic faith was part of my identity growing up, I did not have any Catholic universities on my short list in the fall of my senior year. I was drawn to global issues and thought that studying international relations to prepare for an eventual role in government was the most likely way to feed that interest. Though my father rooted for the Fighting Irish and his Notre Dame degree hung prominently near his desk, Notre Dame wasn't on my list.

Yet in December of my senior year, with college application deadlines looming, I saw the TV movie *Choices of the Heart*. It changed my life trajectory. The movie centered around the civil war in El Salvador and the specific story of three American religious women and a lay missioner working in Catholic ministry there alongside a Salvadoran community where families struggled to meet their basic needs in a context of repression and abuse of human rights. I had until then been only vaguely aware of the conflict and did not know that there were American Catholics who chose to live and work with vulnerable communities as a form of gospel witness. They were doing what Pope Francis has consistently called the church to do: to be in the world, to go to the "peripheries," to demonstrate our faith through our actions and love for those living on the margins. They were striving to be the prophets Romero called all people of Christ to be.

The story of these women—Sister Maura Clarke, Sister Ita Ford, Sister Dorothy Kazel, and lay worker Jean Donovan—appeared on my television because they were Americans brutally murdered for their defense of the community they served in El Salvador. *Choices of the Heart* brought this story to the American public's attention and to me as a teenager in suburban New York. But, of course, it told a universal story of systemic injustice and abuse of power as well as a story of individual Catholics devoting their talents to combat these evils. That same year St. Oscar Arnulfo Romero was assassinated while celebrating mass—at the moment of consecration—for his bold condemnation of human rights violations and a repressive government. The commitment by the women and the bishop to accompany impoverished communities and devote their lives to social justice awoke in me not only a thirst for justice and contributing to change but a desire to go deeper into the gospel foundations of this call to action. And the particular example of Jean Donovan, the lay woman, awakened in me a recognition that someone like me could take up this kind of work in Catholic ministry.

Reflecting on what I learned from that movie about my faith motivations and knowing my father's experience at Notre Dame inspired me to apply. It was one of the first times that I explicitly thought about the hand of the Holy Spirit at work in my life. Opportunities abounded at Notre Dame to study theology and learn about and take part in the church's social justice work. As I learned more about Catholic social teaching concepts, such as the preferential option for the poor, solidarity, and the common good, I learned more about poverty and the church's work to address its symptoms and the root causes. Over my time there my interest in international issues shifted away from diplomacy and statecraft toward service, and away from capital cities toward people and communities on the "peripheries."

A path opened up: After graduation I spent a year in Puerto Rico supporting community-based programs focused on education and economic development. From there, I went to New York City to run an afterschool tutoring program on the Lower East Side and began a master's program at Columbia. The pull of international work remained strong for me, and Columbia had a program focused on global development. I had internalized a faith-driven desire to be of service to others by this time. I also recognized that to be effective, I needed something to offer beyond my desire to do good in the world.

In my last semester of the two-year program I was sipping a coffee in the student lounge when my program adviser found me. "I've been looking for you," he said. "A recruiter is coming to campus to conduct screening interviews for an internship for an international nonprofit." The organization was CRS. I'd never heard of it. But even though the name wasn't familiar to me, by then I was becoming more attuned to what the Holy Spirit was showing me. This one was obvious: a Catholic organization that did the international work I was interested in. Upon graduation from Columbia, I packed my bags and tearfully parted from my family and community to my first assignment for CRS: in El Salvador.

In my third year in El Salvador a call was made for staff interested in supporting an urgent humanitarian response in

Angola, a southern African country besieged by a deadly civil war. CRS needed staff to set up and carry out a lifesaving relief operation in a city where hundreds of thousands of people were suffering from severe food shortages. I felt called to raise my hand, having little idea of what I was getting myself into. The experience changed my life. I discovered that I was calm under pressure, could adapt to the unexpected, could mobilize people quickly toward a common goal—delivering food assistance to desperate people in very precarious situations—in a complex, fluid environment; and could make good decisions with limited information.

Responding to the call to serve in Angola set me on a path over the following decade to devote myself to CRS's emergency programs. In addition to providing on-the-ground surge support and advice to colleagues in countries experiencing natural disasters and violent conflicts, I sought to drive change within CRS and our sister organizations to improve the overall quality of our emergency programs and operations. It was deeply challenging work—notably in violent conflicts where it was clear that politics and the control of resources were the root causes of untold suffering. I have struggled at times with fear and a feeling of inadequacy in the face of enormous need, yet I never doubted how important this work was from a most basic human perspective. The inherent God-given dignity of fellow human beings was under assault. While it was horrifying to be so powerless to stop the fighting, it was clear that our emergency efforts were vital for people's survival—nourishment for their physical well being, as well as an expression of solidarity and compassion for our shared humanity.

The urgency of this work challenged me to understand how to use all that I had been blessed with for a larger purpose. I learned to put my faith into action to drive change and answer the call of my faith to love my neighbor as myself, whether that neighbor is across the street or on the other side of the globe.

When I was younger, I thought about what I wanted to be. But, as I think about it now, it wasn't so much *what* I wanted to be as *who* I wanted to be. I wanted to be someone who applied my skills, experience, gifts, and talents to a greater purpose than myself: to be an instrument of change and plant my stake where the Holy Spirit was calling me.

I have been at CRS for almost three decades now. I have held many different roles, all challenging me to stretch and grow in service to our mission. I have witnessed how critical character is to leadership, both in my actions and my observations of others. As a leader I have learned to be intentional as I seek to embody authenticity and credibility. I believe in demonstrating clear motivations and commitment, delivering on what is promised, prioritizing teamwork and sharing credit, seeing the big picture, and being willing to make hard decisions and owning them. I know how much more we learn when we acknowledge when we don't know what we don't know. And I am constantly inspired by the incredible passion, varied experiences, and deep expertise of my diverse colleagues from around the world.

Hearing God's call took me on a path I could have never imagined—from growing up in a big family on a long, wide suburban New York street to every corner of the globe. That call took me to Notre Dame, where I explored my faith and purpose. It took me to community-based work and daily connections with individuals and their inherent human dignity, no matter the setting and circumstances. It took me to graduate school and onward to CRS—and almost three decades of mission-driven work to meet immediate needs while addressing the root causes of poverty, injustice, and conflict. Ultimately, it has brought together my professional expertise and skills with a faith-filled call to action, motivating me to this day.

Throughout my life I have felt the hand of God guiding me. At times I may have been more or less openhearted and disposed to feel for and recognize that hand. I'm a work in progress, as we all are. I consider myself extremely fortunate for the professional and spiritual growth opportunities that abound in my work. I can lend my talents to a church ministry, catalyzing transformational change in a very broken world. I can see and experience the role of my faith in the world, for which I am grateful beyond words.

22

Kerry Alys Robinson

Executive Partner and Founding Director, Leadership
Roundtable, Washington, DC

Kerry Alys Robinson is the founding executive director and partner for global and national initiatives at Leadership Roundtable and executive director of the Opus Prize Foundation. Kerry has been a lifelong member of the Raskob Foundation for Catholic Activities and FADICA (Foundations and Donors Interested in Catholic Activities). Since 1990, she has been an adviser to and trustee of more than twenty-five national and international grantmaking foundations and charitable nonprofits. Prior to Leadership Roundtable, Kerry served as the director of development for Saint Thomas More Catholic Chapel and Center at Yale University, where she led a successful $75 million capital campaign to expand Catholic life on campus. An ardent advocate for the role of women and young adults in the church, Kerry is a mentor and co-founder of ESTEEM, a national young adult leadership formation program. A frequent writer and international speaker, Kerry is the prize-winning author of *Imagining Abundance: Fundraising, Philanthropy and a Spiritual Call to Service* (Liturgical Press, 2014). She is a graduate of Georgetown and Yale and the recipient of six honorary doctorates. She and her husband, Dr. Michael Cappello, have two children, Christopher and Sophie.

◇◇◇◇◇◇◇◇◇◇◇◇◇◇◇

For as long as I have been aware, I have loved the church and held its potential in the highest esteem. Its explicitly religious mission has formed the person I am. That it is the largest humanitarian network in the world renders me forever committed to its health and vitality.

This is neither blind love nor infatuation, but love borne of time and gratitude and prayer. The more I am engaged in the life of the church, the more I become aware of its history, its mission, its ministries, and its potential. I am aware and in awe of the role women have played in the life of the church, beginning with the moment in time when all of Christianity rested on the faithful, courageous witness of one woman, Mary Magdalene. The church has ennobled me, and at times broken my heart. From the age of fourteen my whole life has been dedicated to serving and strengthening the church.

I first fell in love with the church because of my exposure to it at a very young age through the Raskob Foundation for Catholic Activities. Five generations of our family have served the church through the instrument of this philanthropic foundation. In 1945, our great-grandparents, Helena and John Raskob, established the foundation with two intentions. They wanted all of the foundation's resources to be used exclusively to support the Catholic Church throughout the world, and they wanted their children and descendants to be stewards of the foundation's resources. All participation is voluntary, non-remunerative, and understood to be a serious commitment of time, focus, and engagement in the church's life.

Today there are nearly one hundred members, all descendants of Helena and John, actively engaged in the work of the Raskob Foundation. It has been an uncommon privilege to serve the church in this way, with the unanticipated, beneficial consequence of evangelization for our family. Part of the reason so many family members are Catholic and remain Catholic is because we have a family culture that prizes entrusting the youngest adult members of our family with meaningful leadership on behalf of the foundation. I was in my early twenties when first elected to the board.

As a child I was drawn to women role models whose faith mattered deeply to them, women who had dedicated their lives to ministry and pastoral care and education and social justice. I observed that while these childhood heroines often bore witness to the worst of what humankind does to one another and to our planet, there was a palpable sense of joy about them. Their lives were imbued with purpose and meaning. I admired their faith, their freedom, and their joy.

At the Raskob Foundation we have also seen tremendous challenges facing the church and have been brought up to believe that we have an obligation to help solve those challenges, regardless of how difficult or seemingly insurmountable they may be. Difficult never means impossible.

These have not been easy years to be Catholic as we confront the crisis of clergy sexual abuse, deep divisions within the church, and fractured trust in church leadership, replete with clericalism, sexism, and poor stewardship. I firmly believe, however, that women hold the key to positive managerial reform, the restoration of trust in the church and church leadership, and that now is precisely the time when the church most needs women and what women uniquely have to offer.

The best advice I can offer in times of anguish when the institutional church fails to live up to its potential or manifests ignoble qualities—clericalism, arrogance, fear, secrecy, sanctimony, prejudice, sexism, or mediocrity—comes from my teacher and spiritual director, a beloved Sister of Mercy, Margaret Farley. She said, "Remember what it is you most love about the church and membership in it. Name what you love. Claim what you love. It will provide ballast to allow you to navigate with fidelity and focus when you are disappointed and discouraged." I have taken this advice to heart and highly recommend the discipline.

My list is long and wide. I love Catholic social justice teaching, our church's rich intellectual tradition, sacramental life and imagination, mercy, the Eucharist, the primacy of conscience, prayer and transcendence, forgiveness, the preferential option for the poor and most vulnerable, the injunction to be Christlike. I love that wherever there is human suffering in this world, the church is at the vanguard of providing relief, promoting justice, and advocating for peace. I love the church's aesthetic history expressed in art, architecture, music, and literature. I am daily grateful for Pope Francis. I am grateful that he is on the global stage restoring our faith in humankind by his integrity and mercy. I love that Pope Francis has given us *Laudato Si'* and *Fratelli Tutti,* which provide people of good will a seminal roadmap to care for our common home and one another. And in my grief over losing my closest friend, a Catholic priest, I am grateful more than I can say for our church's articulation of the communion of saints, the conviction of eternal life, the fact that love doesn't end with death. I am reminded of Msgr. Geno Walsh's famous injunction. "Followers of Jesus are promised two things: Your life will have meaning, and you will live forever. If you get a better offer, take it!"

My involvement with our family's foundation led me to meet other families similarly interested in supporting the church. In order to be better informed about the needs of the church and to provide opportunities to collaborate on funding, we formed FADICA. My father, Peter S. Robinson, served as FADICA's founding president. His successor, Frank Butler, was my mentor, which provided me the opportunity to quite literally grow up in this remarkably generous, thoughtful, and dedicated extended philanthropic family.

A small group of my women colleagues in Catholic philanthropy and I have had the rare privilege to meet privately with cardinals all over the world, but especially in Rome. The purpose of our meetings is specific in its simplicity: to discuss the role of women in the church and opportunities to elevate women to positions of meaningful leadership throughout the church and in the Roman Curia.

My women colleagues and I care deeply about the church and represent families with decades of service to the global church. We have studied Catholic theology at the master's and doctoral levels, immersed ourselves in ecclesiology and canon law, raised our children in our faith, and dedicated our lives to serving the church. And because we are radically dedicated to helping the church thrive, we pay particular attention when the church fails to live up to its potential or manifests ignoble qualities: arrogance, clericalism, or poor management. When these qualities fracture trust, alienate people hungry for the gospel, compromise sacramental life, diminish the church's prophetic voice in the public square, and result disproportionately in women and young adults turning away from the church, we are heartbroken and angry for such poor stewardship.

In our meetings with Vatican officials we have been impassioned advocates for women religious. Women religious have been center stage as part of the most compelling, courageous, and effective ministries globally. Promoting, celebrating, and expressing gratitude for their lives, leadership, and example are right and just.

Responding to the sexual-abuse crisis and advocating for the role of lay leadership, and frankly, especially women in the church, have been a central component of my work on behalf of the church all my adult life.

I would have been content to dedicate my entire professional life to the activity of philanthropy, helping funders and foundations make sound investments in people and social enterprises. Philanthropy sounds easy, even luxurious, but anyone who has ever attended to philanthropy seriously knows how demanding and exacting it can be. There are inherently limited resources to extend, always more opportunity and need than available resources to offer. Consequently, the dominant challenge for the dedicated philanthropist is to be strategic, set priorities, exercise effective due diligence, maximize the impact of the grant investment, and measure impact. No easy feat made even more difficult by having to turn down inherently worthy proposals and applicants in favor of those that will be funded. Yet, even so, I vastly preferred the role of grantmaker to its corollary: fundraiser. All of that changed the day I found myself cast in a most unlikely role: director of development for Saint Thomas More Catholic Chapel and Center at Yale University, charged with leading a $75 million capital campaign.

I worked in genuine partnership for ten years with my wonderful friend and colleague Fr. Bob Beloin, Catholic chaplain at Yale. Our commitment was to bring a Catholic intellectual and spiritual center of consequence to fruition on the campus of one of the world's greatest universities and to raise the bar of Catholic campus ministry across the country and world. Our work together was the most profound experience of lay-clergy collaboration that I have ever had.

Nothing in our lifetime was more damaging, discrediting, heartbreaking, or shocking about the church than the abuse revelations brought to light and public consciousness in 2002, halfway through our work together.

It would have been tempting to admit our lack of culpability in the crisis and do nothing. Tempting, but not faithful. We knew that to do nothing is to be complicit. Instead, we hosted a three-day conference entitled "Governance, Accountability, and the Future of the Catholic Church" to examine the underlying conditions that may have contributed to the crisis with a view to making a meaningful and positive contribution to our church. On Yale's campus we hosted five hundred people over three days, featuring thirty nationally recognized speakers. The subject matter was wrenching, and yet everyone left hopeful. We all belonged to the church. This was *our* church. Listening to victim-survivors was the first step, understanding the problems at hand was the second step, committing to being part of the solution was the third step, acting on that commitment was the fourth step.

Three months later I met Geoff Boisi, an extraordinary leader and visionary, world renowned for his financial and investment acumen, who would go on to found Leadership Roundtable and ask me to serve as its founding director.

Leadership Roundtable is a network of senior-level leaders from all walks of life, all of whom are Catholic and committed to making a meaningful contribution to the church. These women and men bring decades of successful leadership, problem-solving ability, managerial expertise, financial acumen, sophisticated command of technology, and capabilities in marketing and communications. They value the church and want it to be strengthened. They yearn to contribute to the restoration of trust that had been so painfully shattered by the sexual-abuse crisis. They want to help usher in a new culture predicated on ethics, transparency, accountability, competency, and justice. They want a church worthy of their children and grandchildren. Since 2016, I have had the privilege of serving as the global ambassador for Leadership Roundtable, offering our resources to benefit the global church.

Lay leadership is essential. Laity, with exceptional managerial expertise and experience, lay women and men of integrity and exemplary character and reputation, must be enlisted to work with church leaders.

In troubled days of prayer about the crisis and how to ensure we are all an effective part of the solution, I asked a close friend of mine, "How does one replenish the reservoir of hope and dedication and faith in the midst of the shame and anguish of the unfolding abuse crisis?" We could pose the same question as we see young adults and women leaving our church. My friend's response was wise: "Pray with the image of the women standing by the cross. Pray with the image of the women giving witness to the resurrection. Scripture describes it as their 'fear giving way to a mounting sense of joy.'"

We are nothing if not a paschal people. Deep within the Catholic imagination is the conviction that out of suffering and death comes new life. Now is the perfect moment for women, with men, to bear witness to the signs of new life for the church and for the world.

23

Julie Sullivan

President, University of St. Thomas,
Minneapolis, Minnesota

Julie Sullivan is the first lay person and woman to serve as president of the University of St. Thomas, the largest private university in Minnesota and a top-20 national Catholic university. Sullivan is a dynamic leader with an entrepreneurial spirit and a passion for creating opportunity and economic inclusion through education. Under her leadership St. Thomas has innovated in academic programs and grown in stature during an uncertain time in higher education. Sullivan served as executive vice president and provost at the University of San Diego (2005–13) after an extensive career as a professor and academic leader at the University of California, San Diego (2003–5) and the University of North Carolina at Chapel Hill (1987–2003), where she was Ernst and Young Distinguished Professor and senior associate dean at the Kenan-Flagler Business School. Sullivan has decades of public company and nonprofit board experience and currently serves on the boards of TCF Financial Corp., Loyola University Chicago, Catholic Charities, Minnesota Business Partnership, Greater MSP, and the Ciresi Walburn Foundation for Children. She also is a member of Women Corporate Directors and Minnesota Women's Economic Roundtable. A Florida native, Sullivan has three degrees from the University of Florida, including a PhD in business.

◇◇◇◇◇◇◇◇◇◇◇◇◇◇◇

Who am I? I am a teacher. As a young child I did not play doctor or house. I played school and coaxed my younger brother into being my pupil. I love teaching. I relish breaking things down into smaller pieces and showing how the pieces fit together. Perhaps, from a visual perspective, this is why I enjoy jigsaw puzzles. Education has been a central part of my entire life. After starting kindergarten at age five, I went straight through school (other than summer jobs and a few months of full-time internships) to finish my PhD and accept my first job as a university professor at age twenty-six. When I started teaching at the university level, I sometimes felt as though I had left my body and was watching someone else in front of the class.

Education is hope. It is the lever that unlocks our potential and helps us understand one another, play a constructive role in society, and contribute to its common good. I learned the importance of educational opportunities at an early age. When I was in seventh grade, my math teacher gave me the textbook and told me to work on my own. When I finished the book by midyear, she said, "You don't need to learn any more math. Instead of coming to math class the rest of the year, I would like for you to assist the remedial reading teacher during this class period." It shocked me to discover that there were children my age still struggling to read, and I spent the rest of the year enjoying reading to and with them. That summer the reading teacher asked me to assist him in teaching Head Start. Again, I became acutely aware of the inequities in our educational opportunities when I handed a young boy a banana, and he handed it back because he had never seen a banana and did not know what to do with it.

Despite my intense passion for education and teaching, I didn't always know I wanted to be an educator. I graduated after eleventh grade from high school in a small town in Florida. There was no college-prep program, and I had run out of classes to take. I entered the University of Florida as a first-generation college student, and while I had never earned a grade below an A, I had no idea how to select a major. I started in pre-med because I thought this was a major for someone who earned good grades, and I had had a lot of positive experiences with physicians, having grown up as a child with severe asthma and allergies. I quickly learned, however, that I was not good with my hands (sewing on a button was a challenge for me), and manual dexterity is essential for physicians. When I asked my father for advice, he said, "I don't care what you major in, as long as you can support yourself when you finish." So, after a wide-ranging exploration of other majors, I ended up selecting accounting. I had always been good at math, had a logical mind, and knew that there would be a job in the end.

During my junior year I interned in the audit and tax departments at Ernst & Young (then Ernst & Whinney). I discovered I enjoyed tax research and planning work (it was like a puzzle) and did not have the same affinity for audit work. During my senior year I received several job offers, requiring me to start in audit. I was told that I could not begin in tax without a master's degree in tax. So, I stayed at the University of Florida and pursued my master's. (So much for Dad's advice. He turned out to be very supportive, however.) During my master's program I worked as a teaching assistant for a professor of large lecture sections in introductory accounting. I had returned to my roots as a teacher and loved it. I quickly decided to continue once again in school (my poor father!) and pursued a PhD at the University of Florida.

My educational and career choices have always been heavily determined by external forces, which I firmly believe are guided by the hand of God. I have actively applied for multiple jobs only twice in my life, once with accounting firms at the end of my bachelor's degree when God led me back to teaching, and once when I finished my PhD and applied for my first university teaching position. After that, through the grace of God, jobs found me at the right time, primarily at times when I was ready to learn and grow in a new way.

After teaching at the University of Oklahoma for four years, I was invited to teach at the University of North Carolina in Chapel Hill for a year as a visiting professor. I loved Chapel Hill and knew I wanted to raise my children and develop as a scholar there. I began praying every morning as I walked the long distance from my assigned parking lot to my office, and by the middle of the year, I was invited to remain as a permanent faculty member. I enjoyed fifteen more years there, matured as a teacher and scholar, and discovered and honed my administrative leadership skills. Nevertheless, I was surprised when asked to take on my first full-time administrative role as senior associate dean of the business school. When I asked, "Why me?" the answer was interesting. I was told that my name had come up most frequently when the faculty were asked whom they would most trust to evaluate them. While I found this flattering, I also knew it would be a big responsibility to fulfill this trust. I was in that role for five years. I grew most from my opportunities to work with a visionary leader, foster global partnerships, and learn from my colleagues across all the disciplines in the business school, as well as from our myriad external supporters.

In 2003, I joined my husband at the University of California San Diego and assisted in creating a new business school. While it was extremely rewarding to create something from scratch, it quickly became evident that I needed to find my own career path in San Diego. One evening I was invited by a very active Catholic woman and friend in the community to a dinner party for some female leaders. I was seated next to the president of the University of San Diego (USD), a school about which I knew little. At the end of the evening she said to me, "You know, my provost position is open." I later learned that she meant to say, "business school dean position." However, God works in mysterious ways. I didn't know what a provost did. I discreetly contacted the search consultant for this position, and after lengthy conversations, we agreed that this would be a good fit for me.

I converted to Catholicism as an adult. Although my mother had attended parochial schools for a few years as a child, I had not. My job as provost at USD was my first experience with Catholic education, and I fell in love with it immediately. With my puzzle fetish, I felt like the missing piece had been added. Reason without faith missed a huge part of how I had always lived my life. I also was very attracted to the opportunity to infuse the educational mission with the principles of Catholic social teaching, particularly the respect for the God-given dignity of every human person and the concept of solidarity or recognition that we are all interdependent and bound by bonds of reciprocity. I connected these principles to the Ashoka changemaking movement that was occurring at the time and thereby found a larger community of universities and colleagues all working to advance the common good.

During my eighth year at USD I was contacted repeatedly by a search consultant and chair of the committee searching for a new president for the University of St. Thomas in Minnesota. In the beginning it was quite easy for me to rebuff these invitations to explore this position. I did not want to leave San Diego for multiple reasons: my husband's career, our new home, and the impending birth of our oldest grandson. However, I knew the trajectory of my learning and growing in my job at USD had slowed, and I had always advised others that this is when you know it is time to change jobs. But move to Minnesota? Remember, I was a Florida girl living in southern California, with little to no knowledge of the University of St. Thomas or the Twin Cities of Minneapolis and St. Paul. Of course, God always has had a much better imagination than I do.

After doggedly persistent requests, I finally agreed to meet with the search committee with the agreement that it was simply to share my experiences at USD. Of course, it quickly turned into an interview, and the more I got to know the St. Thomas trustees, faculty, and staff on the committee, the more impressed

I was with the university and their commitment to it, as well as with the Twin Cities community. During one conversation with the search committee I repeatedly asked whether this Catholic university, founded in 1885 as an all-male institution, became coeducational in 1977, had only fourteen previous presidents, all of whom were priests, was ready for a lay person as president. "If the community is not ready for a lay person," I said, "this will not work for the new president or the university." I repeatedly asked for reassurance that the community was ready to accept a lay leader. Finally, a member of the search committee, a woman of similar stature, intellect, age, and accomplishment as the late US Supreme Court Justice Ruth Bader Ginsburg, pounded her small fist on the table and said, "You haven't even asked about being the first woman president." I jokingly (but erroneously) replied, "I figure if they get over the fact that I am not a priest, they will get over the fact that I am not a man." I did not fully appreciate the importance of her question.

However, soon after assuming the role, I quickly learned how important this was to the community. Administrators, faculty, staff, students, and friends were ready, and they went out of their way to tell me how pleased they were that the university had chosen a woman president. Female students and employees pointed out the importance of being a role model and demonstrating that this position was attainable for women. Male employees and alumni also spoke of how proud they were that their university was open to selecting a female leader.

In closing, my life has been guided by the grace of God. I recall being impressed many decades ago by St. Augustine's advice that we should pray like it all depends on God and work like it all depends on us. Thus, my career goal has been to learn and grow continuously, primarily through constantly seeking opportunities to learn from as many people and experiences as possible. My work is to get myself ready always and ask God to find the communities and organizations that are ready for me.

I have been so fulfilled by my current role because I know it is where God intends for me to be.

Where along the way did I go from being a teacher to becoming a leader? I didn't. I am and have always been both. The skills and goals are fundamentally the same—to inspire people and organizations to do more than they think they can and to assist and support them as they do so.

24

Ana Ventura Phares

*(Retired) Executive Director, Catholic Charities,
Diocese of Monterey, California*

Ana Ventura Phares served on the board of Catholic Charities, Diocese of Monterey, for seven years prior to serving as the executive director from 2018 to 2021. Ana grew up mostly on the Central Coast, where her father worked in the agricultural industry in Salinas and the Imperial Valley of California. She recalls how her parents expected all six of their children to go to college. She received her bachelor's degree from Santa Clara University and her juris doctorate from Thomas Jefferson School of Law. Upon graduation from law school and passing the California bar exam, she worked as an attorney and directing attorney for California Rural Legal Assistance, while also providing a Spanish weekly radio show about legal issues facing the working poor. She was also active in improving voting rights in Monterey County. She then worked in Santa Cruz County Government for twenty-two years as the equal employment opportunity officer. Along the way, Ana noticed how politics made a difference in the way things got done in the community. After serving on the Library and Planning Commission, she was elected Watsonville City Council member and then mayor of Watsonville, the first Mexican American woman to hold the post. She brought a background in human resources, equity and diversity, nonprofits, government, law, and civic participation. She has served on many community boards over the past thirty years and retired from Catholic Charities to care for her father. Ana lives in California with her husband. They have two adult children.

◇◇◇◇◇◇◇◇◇◇◇◇◇◇

I began to serve as the executive director of Catholic Charities, Diocese of Monterey, in California, in 2018. Before serving in this capacity, I served on the Board of Directors for seven years and served as interim director of family services while the organization recruited for a permanent hire. In 2009, a dedicated community leader, Martina O'Sullivan, asked if I would consider joining the board of directors for Catholic Charities. I knew Martina from the circle of women who supported me while I served on the Watsonville City Council in the early 2000s. Martina had served as the executive director in the early 1990s before going on to work for Dominican Hospital for many years. After retiring, she returned to serve as a board member. I give thanks for Martina O'Sullivan's mentorship. She is one of the main reasons I am serving as a leader in this diocese and this community at this unprecedented time. In this position not only am I leading our excellent and dedicated team, but I am also part of community groups that work together to serve those most in need and advocate on their behalf to those with the political power to address the roots of poverty and promote healthier communities for all.

I always loved our Catholic Church but never knew I could be a leader in the church. I thought the only vocation for a woman was that of being a nun. That is what we learn, right? As a girl I wanted to help people and was not afraid to speak up, whether it was helping my parents with translations or helping my dad negotiate the sale price of a refrigerator. My father, a smart man, was only able to attend sixth grade in Mexico, but he had a sister who was able to attend college and become a teacher. I think this helped him realize that women are smart.

He always asked his six children what their goals were and which college they would attend. Well, in some ways, just to have him stop asking, in high school I let him know that I would become a lawyer to help farmworkers. All my life I saw my father work six days a week in the agricultural fields. Yet, by learning English and using his skills as a natural leader, he was promoted many times and completed his career at seventy as the vice president of harvesting. As a girl I saw and appreciated the hard work of farmworkers, and I specifically recall him saying to me, "You might want to help them because not too many people do." He had planted the seed, and it took. My awesome mother raised her children with a perfect balance of care and wisdom, especially as we traveled up and down California in the early years. Navigating schools every six months was probably challenging for her, but I never heard her complain. She had married my dad at seventeen and moved to this country. Although she was not familiar with the ways of the United States, she quietly approved of all our opportunities and freedoms and would often say, "Why not? You can do it; you are here with all these options."

I attended Santa Clara University in California and majored in Spanish literature. I felt it very important to learn to read, write, and speak Spanish and be fully proficient in both English and Spanish. At Santa Clara, I quickly made friends with students in the Mexican American/Chicano (MECha) Student Association. In this wonderful group I learned to address and solve issues in our college community and, of course, to support each other in this new environment. After college I attended Thomas Jefferson Law School in San Diego and graduated in four years, working part time and enjoying sunny San Diego. However, the California bar exam was an obstacle. I like to say that I failed as many times as John F. Kennedy Jr.—and on the fourth time, we both passed. I kept trying, which I now realize is a good trait to have as a leader because you must always have hope, maintain positivity, and try new ways to continue the work at hand. I have my parents to thank for this because they were instrumental in supporting me and believing that I could achieve this goal. I thank my mother at this point in my life because she advised me to return home to help in the upcoming Catholic Spanish cursillo while I studied one more time. She is the wisest woman I know. I followed her advice and studied while attending the cursillo prep meetings. The organizers asked me to present the topic "faith vs. fear" for the next cursillo weekend. After preparing for both, would you believe that the exam results were mailed the same weekend as the cursillo? On the day we welcomed the community to the new cursillistas, my parents brought the letter (already opened) with the positive results. I must say that at this time I also met the man I was to marry three years later. God and my mother had their plans, and I am grateful to both! I participated in several more cursillos and to this day maintain close bonds with many from that time.

Well, my good fate continued because, soon after that, I went to work for California Rural Legal Assistance in Salinas, California, helping low-income people, mostly farmworkers, with eviction prevention, unemployment, and other housing issues. I also provided training on tenants' rights and had a radio show in Spanish where I presented various legal topics to help people with the subjects mentioned above. These five years developed my public speaking in two languages and my advocacy work with others in the community. I also became directly involved in politics and was one of the plaintiffs in the successful voting rights case that finally allowed district elections in the County of Monterey.

On my last year at California Rural Legal Assistance I read an article in the Santa Cruz newspaper announcing that the equal employment officer (EEO) of the county was quitting because, as he put it, "the board of supervisors cared more about salamanders than people of color." His boldness intrigued me into finding out about the position, and of course, I applied. I decided that I wanted to be part of the solution to ensure that qualified people of all backgrounds were not discriminated against. I knew that feeling. It reminded me of when I asked my high school counselor about college, and he responded, "Why? Mexican girls don't attend college." When I shared this with my father, he quickly said, "Find another counselor." I inquired at the counseling office, and sure enough, another counselor agreed to meet with me, said I had good grades, was involved in activities, and that "I would do great things after college." I am thankful for my counselor, Mr. Sullivan. He helped many smart Mexican students apply for college.

In 1994, I started working as the analyst for the Equal Employment Office. After one year I was promoted to the EEO position, which included ensuring that the Americans with Disabilities Act of 1990 was enforced. It was an exciting job because I worked with each department (from the Sheriff's Office to Public Works) on how best to promote equal employment, figure out how to serve the community better, and recruit persons based on those business needs. I also conducted investigations; taught employees about civil rights, EEO, and the prevention of harassment; and worked with employees regarding disability-related accommodations. I created cultural competency plans with the collaboration of their managers to develop action steps to serve their customers, constituents, and employees more efficiently and appropriately.

At this same time my career path turned to community service. While speaking at a town hall meeting on improving educational opportunities for migrant students, a Latino Watsonville council member present at the meeting told me that I could do well by serving on one of the city commissions. I said yes to that call and ended up serving on the Library and Planning Commissions before running for City Council and serving eight years. During that time I served on many committees that allowed me to represent the community that is not usually at the table. During these years I learned to become confident in my voice and explain why I decided one way or another. I also grew to enjoy working with others with similar goals to achieve good things such as parks, libraries, schools, safe neighborhoods, housing, and improved outreach and engagement with the entire community, including seniors, families, and the Latino Spanish-speaking community. Those were phenomenal years of community organizing and collaborating with diverse groups to reach common ground. I also learned the bigger picture of power by participating with other city council members from around the state to advocate for our communities. I truly appreciate my husband and my mom, who together supported me while raising my family. Because of them, I was successful in having two careers at the same time.

Five years ago, at fifty-five, I retired from my EEO position to take a break and perhaps find another calling. At that time, as I mentioned above, I was serving on the board of directors for Dominican Hospital, sponsored by the Dominican Sisters. The president of the board, Sister Janet Capone, and I had a good conversation about how to know your calling. Little did I know that God was leading me to work for Catholic Charities. She said, "Where is the need? Where can God use your gifts?"

When the board asked me to serve as the interim director, I found that I loved the work because it was all my past positions rolled into one incredible job with Jesus in the middle. To work for the social justice arm of the Catholic Church with the mission to serve the most vulnerable and in dire need of help and hope seemed perfect for me. I had been looking for a job where I could serve God, use my skills from my work and political service, and here it was, in my home region. A few board members hoped that I would love the work, and after a few interviews and a review of my work as interim, we both said yes to this new partnership.

With this year of the pandemic and wildfires, what I have learned the most is doing your work but trusting God completely to help you and your ministry carry out the work. With staff who pursue excellence in our mission, we have done more than the imaginable by listening to one another, praying together, supporting one another, following our intuition and ideas, and solving challenges. As our chairman, Bishop Danny, said to me, "Jesus won't let you down in this work if you carry on and trust him." Mary of Miracles and Padre Pio became our patron saints this past year because we needed to carry out amazing new work and be at two places at one time.

There are many skills necessary to lead in this ministry. Aside from understanding the complexities of nonprofit management, there are more that come to mind: Believe in the mission wholeheartedly and be prepared, pray, and have confidence that God will help you. Hire smart staff who complement your skills. Be able to multitask or juggle work. Write and speak well. Have good listening and human-resource-management skills. Have friends to whom you can go for guidance. Have the ability to work with and care about people from all backgrounds. And find joy in the everyday work, find humor, and laugh every day!

25

Kerry Weber

Executive Editor, America *Magazine*

Kerry Weber is an executive editor of *America,* where she has worked since 2009. Kerry is the author of *Mercy in the City: How to Feed the Hungry, Give Drink to the Thirsty, Visit the Imprisoned and Keep Your Day Job* (Loyola Press, 2014), which received a Christopher Award, as well as awards from the Catholic Press Association and the Association of Catholic Publishers. In 2013 she reported from Rwanda as a recipient of a Catholic Relief Services' Egan Journalism Fellowship. She has served on the boards of the Catholic Press Association and the Ignatian Solidarity Network. A graduate of Providence College and the Columbia University Graduate School of Journalism, Kerry has previously worked as an editor for *Catholic Digest,* reporter for a local newspaper, a producer for a diocesan television program, and a special-education teacher on the Navajo Nation in Arizona.

My first memories of a newsroom include the excessive use of intra-office phones, the satisfying *thump* of a rubber stamp on paper, and the consumption of an enormous quantity of fruit snacks. I was five years old, and my mother, a family columnist for the diocesan newspaper in Springfield, Massachusetts, balanced her dual jobs of writer and parent by occasionally bringing me and my younger brother to her office.

My brother and I spent the time calling each other from various extensions and stamping the date in red and black ink on scrap paper. I loved the hum and controlled chaos of a newsroom and felt welcomed by my mother's colleagues. In fact, I felt so at home in this environment, it was only natural when, during high school, I joined the diocesan newspaper staff as well.

I took on the role of reporter and also began work as a producer for the diocesan television news program. I felt excited to once again use the official office phones, but I also found that I enjoyed the responsibility of documenting events, asking questions, and telling stories about local happenings and individuals.

Eventually I headed for Providence College in Providence, Rhode Island, where I earned a BA in English and studied abroad at Blackfriars Hall at Oxford University. In my studies at both of these institutions I gained a deeper understanding of the power of stories, including the written word's ability to incite change, both societal and personal. I had my first chance to truly study the history that has shaped our society's views on race and class, the literature inspired by revolutions, or the theology fueling our care for the poor.

I was still sorting out exactly what I believed in, and why I believed it, and then trying to determine, crucially, what action was required to demonstrate these beliefs. And what I found was that, as it turns out, I wasn't the first person to consider these questions. I got the chance to read books that examined our collective past and that provided meaningful context for our world right now. I was introduced to Aristotle, who theorized that the just person is formed by doing just acts in the way that a just person would do them. I met St. Thomas Aquinas, who apparently was pretty good at asking and answering questions himself, including what it means to be merciful and virtuous, what it means to show pity or charity or justice. I read *Hard*

Times by Charles Dickens and considered the tragedy of poor working conditions and the dangers of taking Utilitarianism too far. I entered into the many mansions of St. Teresa of Avila's *Interior Castle,* in which she argues that the "Lord does not care so much for the importance of our works as for the love with which they are done."

And every summer throughout college I returned to the diocesan office for the chance to work in local Catholic journalism, because I hoped that the work might help to tell another powerful story—that of a community journeying together toward Christ. But, in the meantime, my own journey also included time spent stuffing envelopes for mass mailings and making cold calls for a reader survey. It meant running the teleprompter for live shoots and, occasionally, running the camera for televised mass. It meant covering an elevator blessing and interviewing the bishop. But in between all of that I also got to ask questions of strangers who opened up to me and spoke eloquently and passionately about God at work in their lives.

After graduating from college I served for one year as a volunteer special-education teacher in St. Michaels, Arizona, on the Navajo Nation. Each day was a blessing and a challenge, and my work as a teacher there instilled in me a desire to continue to develop greater kinship with marginalized people and to try to encourage that kinship through my writing. As a journalist, I feel a responsibility to amplify the stories and voices that otherwise might not be heard.

After my volunteer year I had the chance to work as an editor and writer for *Catholic Digest.* During that time I donned scrubs to observe surgeries with Air Force chaplains in training at Wilford Hall Medical Center in San Antonio, Texas. I knelt in a Massachusetts field to aid in the birth of a newborn lamb at a Heifer International farm. I walked with pilgrims to the Basilica of Our Lady of Guadalupe in Mexico City. And I learned that editing is also a form of ministry. I learned that using my own voice to tell stories can be fulfilling, but helping others to develop their own voices through their writing can be just as exciting.

Having grown up in the Catholic press, I left *Catholic Digest* to attend the Columbia University School of Journalism, with the hope of pivoting to more secular topics. But my studies there made me realize the importance of religion coverage and my own passion for it. Although I could cover any topic, I found myself continually drawn to those stories at the intersection of the church and the world, and after graduating I made a deliberate choice to continue my work in the Catholic press, and I jumped at the chance to work for *America*.

I remember flipping through a copy of *America* at a friend's house in high school and thinking that maybe I could work for them someday. Then I flipped to the masthead and saw that it was almost entirely Jesuits; and then I thought, *maybe not*. These days our work is a fruitful collaboration between lay and Jesuit editors, and I'm happy to say I am just one of many more women on the masthead. And I hope that anyone can look through that list of names and feel encouraged by who is represented there.

I am tremendously grateful to be able to do the work that I do at *America*. I believe that both journalism and religion center around our search for answers. As human beings we want to know, and it is a journalist's job to ask, to search, to answer. It is my hope that my work, whether through writing or editing, will prompt readers to think, to feel, and to question for themselves. A big part of my job, as I view it, is to help identify and empower strong voices from all corners of the church who are willing to speak the truth to all corners of the world.

As an editor, I am privileged to work with many talented writers and to help shape the stories they tell. Editing is about humility. It is work that, when done well, goes unnoticed by the readers, and that is how it should be. An editor's work is the work of helping authors sound more like their most authentic self. In this way I hope that my work and the work that we do at *America* is also a way of quietly fostering a conversation among all people of goodwill as we all try to become more authentically who Christ calls us to be. I believe that much of the value of my work lies not in my own tasks or accomplishments but in what my colleagues and I are able to do together.

In his message for World Communications Day in 2013, Pope Benedict wrote that social media need "the commitment of all who are conscious of the value of dialogue, reasoned debate and logical argumentation; of people who strive to cultivate forms of discourse and expression which appeal to the noblest aspirations of those engaged in the communication process." These are lofty words for digital spaces often dominated by cats' pictures.

But he's right. We need that. But how do we actually help to form people capable of entering the digital space in that way? People capable of true charity, hope, and love while in conversation in the digital world or the real one? How do we make sure people are, in fact, entering into conversation at all? How do we keep people from spending all their time scrolling without ever stopping to truly start thinking? My hope is that Catholic publishing can play a role in promoting the value of dialogue and noble discourse, one piece of content at a time.

All people want to be of use. We want to be seen. We want to help, to inform, to be informed, to connect, to feel a little bit less alone in our struggles and joys. Catholic publishing becomes a media ministry for others when it inspires people to read or listen or watch, not just for themselves but because they hope that the content they encounter might transform how they treat others.

Since having my children, I have had to make very deliberate decisions about how I spend my time. I have had to let go of some things I loved to make sure I had time for my family. And in doing this, I have come to realize that words, the reading of them, the writing of them, the editing of them, remain worthy of my time. And not only that, they are crucial to helping build the sort of home and world I want my children to experience.

All too often, whether intentionally or mistakenly, we try to lock God out of our lives, not by becoming atheists, but by refusing to see Christ in those around us. By sometimes arguing, as the apostle Thomas might have, "*This* isn't how I expected God to show up!" Yet the best of what we produce at *America* helps us to acknowledge that God might appear in our lives in unexpected ways and might speak to us through someone very different from ourselves.

We have the opportunity to surprise readers—to offer the work of a fellow person of faith on a different topic or perspective from their usual beat, or to offer a nuanced and thoughtful, and thoughtfully edited, perspective, that can help readers to see all people as, well, people, with depth and complexity.

A good leader should be willing to be surprised. In fact, the element of surprise may be a helpful step toward uniting a sometimes fractured church and world. Surprise is an emotion that disarms. When we are caught off guard, we become vulnerable; and often it is in our most vulnerable times that we are most open to accepting grace and to truly treating one another with mercy, to accepting mercy, to truly being changed, to saying, as Thomas did, "My Lord and my God."

In *Evangelii Gaudium* Pope Francis writes that "an evangelizing community gets involved by word and deed in people's daily lives. . . . An evangelizing community is filled with joy; it knows how to rejoice always. It celebrates every small victory, every step forward" (no. 24).

The words we publish help to shape people's daily lives. Their daily actions. They help us to become like family to one another. In his message for World Communications Day in 2015, Pope Francis described the family as "an environment in which we learn to communicate in an experience of closeness . . . a 'communicating community.'" And so, in the end, the point of what

Catholic authors and publishers do is not to get people to buy millions of books or follow us on social media. (Although we often hope that you do.) The point is to form each other in the gospel, to model dialogue, inform and strengthen faith, making the best use of the many tools that we have today in order to build a "communicating community" of readers and writers and leaders that also feels a lot like a family.

26

Carolyn Y. Woo

(Retired) President and Chief Executive Officer, Catholic Relief Services

Carolyn Woo received her bachelor, master, and PhD degrees at Purdue University, where she also served as a faculty member and administrator from 1981 to 1997. In 1997, Woo joined the University of Notre Dame as Martin J. Gillen Dean of the Mendoza College of Business. During her tenure the undergraduate program earned #1 rankings from *Bloomberg/BusinessWeek* and was consistently noted for its leadership in ethics education. Woo was elected the first female chair of AACSB International (accreditation association for business schools worldwide) and led the launch of the Principles for Responsible Management program with the United Nations. Carolyn then served Catholic Relief Services as CEO from 2012 to 2016. CRS undertakes humanitarian relief and sustainable development in over one hundred countries serving over one hundred million people each year. Carolyn was recognized as one of the five hundred most powerful people on the planet by *Foreign Policy* magazine in 2013 and one of only thirty-three in the category "a force for good." Dr. Woo has logged extensive service on corporate, Catholic, and other non-profit boards. At the Vatican she spoke at the launch of Pope Francis's encyclical *Laudato Si'*, organized two conferences on impact investing, and three CEO dialogues on energy transition. In addition to teaching, research, and leadership awards, Carolyn took first place in the 2013

Catholic Press Association awards for "best regular column—spiritual life." She is the recipient of thirty honorary doctorates. Carolyn is married to Dr. David Bartkus, and they have two sons, Ryan and Justin.

◇◇◇◇◇◇◇◇◇◇◇◇◇◇

Before I was born, my parents were desperately hoping for a boy. Perhaps more so for my mom as she had arrived at an understanding with my father that if the next child were not a son, my father could seek a second wife. At that time in Hong Kong, polygamy was allowed by law and practiced in the Chinese culture. Of the four children my parents had by then, there was only one boy. My father was determined to have two sons: "an heir and a spare." One would be a doctor and the other a lawyer. They would carry on the name and cover the key exigencies of life.

Well, I was not the hoped-for son. Fortunately, my mother soon conceived again and fortune smiled on the family granting us a boy baby. Fulfilling my father's wishes, my two brothers made their careers in the medical and legal professions. The intent for the four daughters was a bit undefined except to marry well. Education was necessary, but university studies and professional training not so much. None of my sisters went to college.

We were a close family with laughter and stories every night at the dinner table. We were not without worries: my father's temper outbursts, gambling, health, and work frustrations; and my mother's adjustment to a Western culture of which she knew little.

Despite the worries, squabbles, and the vicissitudes of life, love blossomed. I learned early that I loved my father very much, not because he was perfect, but because he was family. I sensed that behind his blustery demeanor, he had fears and vulnerabilities. I developed an instinct about people's vulnerabilities and shortfalls and love them more for these.

My care was entrusted to a nanny who joined the family eight years before I was born. Early on, one of my sisters referred to her as Gaga and so we all did. (We had our own Gaga before Lady Gaga!) Our Gaga had steel for her backbone and stopped at nothing for the good of others. She lived by Confucian maxims and cited Chinese folklore to instill the values of filial piety to parents, loyalty to employers and friends, kindness to others, generosity, hard work (actually perfect work), and uncompromising integrity. All these packed into a petite frame that moved from chore to chore from six o'clock in the morning to ten o'clock at night.

Gaga became a servant girl at nine years of age when her mother was widowed and left with the care of four children. Gaga's labor made possible the medicine needed for her baby brother and food for the rest of the family. Her father taught her to read a little before he died, and she picked up the rest standing outside the classroom where her employer's children went to school. From these experiences she mastered sufficient literacy to read a newspaper. Gaga moved with her employers through different parts of China and eventually to Vietnam and Hong Kong during WWII. She was very beautiful; her picture on my mantle would always draw admiration. She rejected the marriage offers that came through her employers to maintain the freedom to earn money for her family.

You would imagine a person who carried the weight of her family since childhood to be bitter and resentful, but not Gaga. Every morning, her first act was to light two joss sticks, kneel on both knees in front of the kitchen window, and bow deeply. For Gaga, the first priority of each day was to thank the heavens and the earth. A profound sense of blessing and abundance filled this servant woman.

When I started preschool, Gaga braided my hair in pigtails and helped me get into my cotton uniform starched to perfect crispness. As she handed me the container with the wetted hand towel, she would say, "Listen and obey your teacher, do not play until you finish your work, do it well, and bring home a rabbit."

If a student were obedient and did good work, the teacher would stamp her report card with the picture of a rabbit for that day. Otherwise, it would be a pig.

After one year of all rabbits, I got my first award for outstanding performance. The memento was a very thin gold medallion with my name and the characters of "perfect conduct" inscribed. Gaga put this on a chain and let me wear it.

In my teens I told Gaga that my English vocabulary would not be good enough to qualify for entry into an American university. She promptly suggested my memorizing the dictionary for an added hour of study each night. Her sense of "can do" became ingrained in me. And of course, the twin engines of that spirit were hard work and duty.

From elementary through high school, I was enrolled at the Maryknoll Sisters' School established by the Maryknoll Sisters of Ossining, New York. They were the first Catholic women missionary order founded in the United States. My school was known for the students' fluency in English, their "with it" style, and their poise in social situations. Students and alumnae are known as "Maryknoll girls" regardless of how old we are.

Through lessons in reading, writing, arithmetic, and biblical knowledge, we mastered not just vocabulary and composition, concepts, and analytics, but developed a sense of personal impact and opportunity. Against the cultural expectations for women, we were taught to form our own ideas, articulate our reasoning, take positions on issues, and act for the common good. We cultivated our voice for ourselves and others. We were encouraged to have professional aspirations and to pursue them.

When we got cocky winning debate competitions against other Chinese students, the Sisters created matches for us with the British boys. Any protestation of unfairness would be lost in the Sisters' efforts to build our courage and break through the limitations we put on ourselves. I was the captain of the debate team tasked with the final summation. On the morning of competitions, I would lose my voice completely. My classmates would come to school ready with honey and other soothing remedies to nurse me back to health and to make sure I would step up.

Hong Kong was an ultra-competitive academic arena where students took public examinations after the sixth and eleventh grades. We were assessed on a curve where only a minority could move forward to the high schools of our choice, and eventually to university. At Maryknoll Sisters' School, in contrast to a rivalrous external culture, we created a spirit of cooperation and mutual assistance. It is ironic that in one of the most competitive environments, I learned about friendship and community. Even today, the Maryknoll girls stay in touch, share advice on anything from cooking to surviving COVID-19, offer shoulders to cry on, and affirm each other. A necessary characteristic I look for in a colleague is the capacity to shine the spotlight on others and work for another's success.

God became real to me because God was real to the Sisters. At certain points the girls wondered why the Sisters would leave America, which we looked up to as a beacon of opportunities and freedom, to come to teach us. Early days of the Maryknoll Sisters in China brought hardships of yellow fever, other diseases, and even imprisonment. It is because, they said, they love God. As my classmates and I grew older, we developed the habit of visiting the chapel during the lunch period. We brought our many worries about our future as children of immigrants, and probably because we were teenagers finding ourselves. Catholic or not, we must have developed from the Sisters a trust in God.

The Sisters, like Gaga, did not easily settle for no as an answer when a need was to be met. They started schools in low-income districts, clinics, hospitals, care centers for the elderly and the disabled. When seed money was needed, they engaged the students in fund drives. They gave up buses and trams to save the fares. One Sister moved on to co-found the Maryknoll Center for

Justice and Peace; another became the liaison for the investigation of the religious women martyred in El Salvador; a number were elected to the order's governing board, while others moved into ghettos to serve and live in solidarity with the poor.

My most valuable lesson from those school years was the connection between faith and joy. The Maryknoll Sisters sparkled with joy, hearty laughs, humor, and fun. Just in case anyone missed the point, Sr. Mary Lou would instruct new friends and students that her surname name "Teufel" rhymes with "joyful." My faith was formed by holy women, spirited giants.

I wanted to study in the United States. After twelve years with the Maryknoll Sisters, having watched thousands of hours of American television and imbibed the spirit of Apollo missions, fights for women's equality, peace, and racial justice, I was hooked.

I was also very concerned about the well being of my elders. My father had no savings; whenever he came into money, it would be spent or gambled away. My mother felt helpless, and Gaga was getting old. I accepted that it was my responsibility to take care of them. I also sensed that I would flourish in the Western style of education and would likely make a better living for my family in America, known in Chinese as the "Gold Mountain." But I had neither money nor a game plan. Research at the United States Information Services (USIS) led to pages of notes on universities from a ten-pound directory. They all seemed enticing and completely out of reach.

Serendipity would intervene as I crossed the path of an economics professor on leave in Hong Kong. On Saturdays, I would go to my big sister Helen's office at Trans World Airlines, where she worked as a secretary. I was the human collator and stapler before the functions were automated. In came this professor who asked about my plans, just to be polite. I told him of my dream to go to college in the United States. He was from Purdue University, a comprehensive university where I could study anything I want. I zeroed in on the information about Purdue in the directory at USIS, dog-eared the page, and took off on flights of adventure with the description of different majors and programs. I memorized the tuition and room and board for foreign students: $800 and $500, respectively, per semester.

I made all the necessary preparations: begged for the fee for the SAT from my mother; raised funds for one year's worth of tuition from my older siblings; procured an airline ticket from my TWA sister; and got my older doctor brother to underwrite one year of my room and board expenses. I budgeted twenty dollars a month for incidentals with aerograms (the cheapest form of international mail) consuming a large percentage. Before my departure, Gaga gave me a thick gold bracelet made of 24–karat gold. It would buy my passage home if things did not work out. Gaga never gave herself an out, but she made sure I had one.

When all the elements came together, I approached my father for permission to pursue my dream. I told him I took care of the expenses as I knew it would be a hardship for him. He was reluctant to let me go because I was a girl and could not possibly handle the hippies of Haight Ashbury, which he had visited the prior year. Except for one sister, all the other siblings had left Hong Kong. I would be the daughter to stay home and keep him and my mother company.

I asked that he let me go and treat me as a son. I would make him proud as a "Woo." I would support him, my mother, and my nanny, accepting the responsibility expected of sons. I did not change my last name to keep that promise.

My father relented and let me go. While visiting me in my first semester at Purdue, he wanted to walk with me to the Physics Building for my 7:30 a.m. calculus class. He was not strong enough for the trek and stopped before we reached the destination. I turned around and saw him on a bench, glasses removed and tears on his face.

During my student years, I sent my father every award notification, certificate, letter of congratulation, and press clipping as my offering. Fortunes had reversed by the time of my graduation, and my father brought the family for the commencement celebrations. Years later, when organizing his personal effects after my father had passed away, I found the scrapbook with all the notices I sent him. The commencement program was turned to the page listing my name. My mother told me that he would often look at these and then press the book on friends when they visited. Today, when I speak at commencement ceremonies, I tell the guests to keep extra copies of the program.

My first year at Purdue was both lonely and exhilarating. For a month I cried in the shower because I missed my family and friends terribly. Knowing I was working against the clock, I signed up for as many courses as my schedule could accommodate. Over two semesters I dropped a movie appreciation class because I could not stay awake at the viewings, and a Russian class because I did not have enough hours to learn the alphabet and practice the pronunciation. I completed the academic year with forty-two credit hours.

St. Thomas Aquinas Center, located in the middle of campus, became my home. Between class and daily mass, I would study in the library downstairs. I signed on as lector and eucharistic minister, and sang with the choir. For study breaks I would attend talks and help out with events. By the end of my first year I was elected secretary of the parish council and served with David Bartkus, the president of the council. David was a fellow daily mass attendee, and we became good friends. Six years later we became best friends in marriage. The day before our wedding I mailed my doctoral dissertation to the faculty committee to keep a promise to myself that I would complete my education before marrying.

The priests and staff of St. Tom's adopted me. I would join them at the lunch table, sharing the treats parishioners had brought. The St. Tom's community invited me home with them during holidays and made me part of their families. The staff made a point to attend academic ceremonies with me to make sure that I, like the other students, had someone cheering for me. Fr. Leo rang the church bells when I defended my dissertation.

I first learned about women's formal leadership in the church from Mary Pat Siczek, who was appointed co-pastor by Fr. Leo Piquet. It was not the shortage of priests that drove the decision, as there were four serving St. Tom's, but the recognition of Mary Pat's gifts and how she could make the place better. That was fifty years ago. Together, they led the center to cultivate an adult faith that kept pace with the intellectual development of the undergraduate and graduate student bodies. I learned about church as community and as one body in Christ from St. Tom's. It was not an intellectual derivation but a lived experience from the hospitality and care I received.

I applied for a full scholarship in my second semester, hoping against hope that someone would want to support an international undergraduate student. I had a shot but a very long one as there were only two such scholarships. International students are often admitted by universities to augment revenues. It is the lowest priority for claiming university resources or development funds.

On the day when the awards were to be announced, I had to make a decision. I could rush over to the International Student Office after class at 11:20 a.m. or go to 11:30 a.m. mass and then wait an hour for the office to reopen at 1:00 p.m. I decided to go to mass for two reasons: (1) to delay getting bad news, as I did not really think I had a chance; and (2) to have a very, very good talk with God. During my hour at church, on my knees, I let God know how unfair it was to be born a girl: to have to work harder, but not necessarily for any tangible result. I did not know what else I could do but go home and hopefully find a path that would allow me to support my family.

I got the scholarship.

In my second year at Purdue there was a knock on the door one evening after dinner. A group of girls rushed in with a rose. I was tapped to be a member of Mortar Board. I had no idea what it meant but later found out that Mortar Board is a prestigious honor society for women leaders. Mary Pat had nominated me. The women were mostly presidents and officers of sororities, clubs, college chapters of professional associations, residence halls, and student government.

Our first meeting was an offsite retreat. I was assigned a cot next to a young woman of great poise and confidence. She had brought along a silk pillowcase and explained that it would prevent her hair from forming knots. I did not feel my dorm-issued pillowcase was lacking until then. In our warmup conversation she spoke of her leadership agenda and asked about mine. I was too embarrassed to admit that I did not know what that was. But I had enough protective instinct to reply that carrying twenty-one credit hours had prevented me from finishing mine.

That evening I went to the Mortar Board adviser and explained that it was a mistake for me to be in Mortar Board. I had no real title (secretary of parish council just did not sound impressive), had not led anything, and never received formal leadership training. And while we were at it, what is a leadership agenda?

The wonderful counselor reassured me that I belonged. My service to St. Tom's was important, and my leadership agenda would be what more St. Tom's could do to serve parishioners and help them grow in their faith. I had some thoughts on that but still did not see myself as a leader. "One day," my counselor said, "you will understand what a leader is and accept yourself as one." I was deeply grateful for this kind woman and her embrace of a young student with no confidence. I burst with joy when she attended the commencement speech I gave at Purdue in 2015. After decades of experience I conclude that "belonging" is overrated as a qualification for leadership.

Purdue continued to fund me through graduate studies. For my PhD, I specialized in an emerging discipline known as strategic management. I worked in industry and consulting for two years afterward, and then decided to return to academia. Purdue welcomed me back as an assistant professor and eventually invited me into academic administration. Twenty-five years after I arrived at Purdue, I left with deep sadness to serve as dean of the business school at Notre Dame.

I initially turned down the invitation from Notre Dame. But one day I stepped out at daily mass and felt that I was staying at Purdue for the wrong reasons. I felt compelled to make the case that faith and business are not opposing forces, but faith enables business to be a force for good. The chair of the Purdue board, president, and provost were all people of deep faith. When they asked what they could do to keep me at the university, I replied that none of us, including me, could do anything as this seemed like the will of God. Fifteen years later CRS beckoned. Again I was reluctant to leave, but eventually I recognized that I would be going home to people who are living the refugee and immigrant experiences that my family went through.

My father passed two years after my completion of the doctorate. He was beyond proud. My mom lived into her eighties, and my nanny was one hundred years old when she passed. Both women converted to Catholicism in their elder years. Dave and I kept my childhood promise that they would be cared for properly.

At my nanny's funeral the parlor was filled with Gaga's nieces, nephews, their spouses and children. Directly or indirectly, all benefited from Gaga's giving all she had to sustain her siblings, their parents. They had great educations and flourished in their careers. Decades ago, the youngest niece, Lily, wanted a piano. Gaga dedicated several months of her salary to purchase a used instrument. Today Lily is a piano teacher and mother of a teen phenom. At fourteen, Gaga's grandniece has mastered the highest levels in piano, violin, and getting there in voice and dance. She is also a gifted athlete, artist, and student. I was shown the picture of a very big table topped with trophies. One servant girl devoted to her family enabled the success of so many.

When I was young, I felt that I carried heavy burdens all on my own. In retrospect, whenever I pray, God sends people. In addition to my family, friends, and Maryknoll Sisters in Hong Kong, I was carried by the St. Tom's community, academic counselors, residence-hall staff, roommates, roommates' families, teachers, major professor and committee members, university administrators, colleagues, program leaders, senior scholars in the profession, executive assistants . . . the list goes on. People did what they could to help me find my way; get access to resources; gain confidence; learn the ropes for teaching, publishing, and administering; be nominated; be comforted; be loved. My husband and sons became my biggest cheerleaders, generously forgiving when work completely consumed my time, attention, and good humor.

"Bidden or not bidden, God is present."[1]

---

[1] "Vocatus atque no vocatus deus aderit." This quotation, inscribed in Latin over the entrance to Carl Jung's house in Kusnacht, is attributed to the Oracle of Delphi.

PART IV

REFLECTIONS ON LEADERSHIP

27

Growing into Leadership

Jennifer Fiduccia

What are the most common misperceptions about women and leadership in Catholic ministries?

While women lead in the church in a multitude of both formal and informal ways, there is still an abundance of misconceptions about women and leadership. Our vocation as Christians comes first from our baptism, as we are called into the threefold ministry of Jesus, to act as priests, prophets, and kings. It is unfortunate that for women, the kingly nature of our baptism and our call to governance as a part of our identity in Christ does not extend to much of the formal leadership structure of the church. It is a misconception that because we are not men, we are not equipped for certain leadership roles. I have heard this justified in several ways, but one of the most frustrating is the fallacy that women are too emotional to lead and are ill-equipped to make financial decisions, lead strategic planning, or take on other rational roles in organizations. In addition, it has been suggested to me that my place is in the home, raising my children, and that I should leave the work of the church to the ordained and religious. Should a woman's vocation be solely tied to her

gender, marital status, or parental status, or should the community find ways to support a woman who is wife, mother, and
called to ministry? When we pray for vocations in a community,
do we pray for vocations with our own narrow view, or do we
pray with the conviction that the Spirit will pour out the gifts
according to need and stretch our imaginations to embrace the
possibility of what new things God is doing?

Another misconception I have encountered as a lay ecclesial
minister is that women who work in the church do not need
to be paid a just wage for their labor if they have a spouse who
is the family's breadwinner. I was once told that I should be
grateful that my husband allows me to work outside the home
and that part of my stewardship to the church is accepting a
lower wage. (That particular finance director added, "And besides, you don't need the money—you have a husband.") Just
compensation for labor is part of our rich tradition of Catholic
social teaching. Male or female, married or unmarried, wanting
or well off, employees of the church deserved to be paid just
wages for their work.

From the time of Jesus, women have been entrusted with
proclaiming the gospel, leading communities, and doing much of
the "work" of the church. To assume, then, that they are not cut
out for leadership at any and every level is preposterous. Women
have acted as de facto leaders in the church for hundreds of years,
often ensuring its longevity and success.

*How do you understand or exercise the role of leadership? How has
your experience of being a woman affected your understanding or
exercise of leadership in the church?*

The role of leadership as a Christian is to be a servant first. There
is no room for ego, personal agenda, exclusion of others, pride,
or arrogance. To exercise this role is to lead from wherever I find
myself, which means putting myself in the service of others. It

means looking at what the needs of the individual or the community are and considering how my giftedness and ability intersect with those needs. It often also means putting aside what I *want* to do in favor of what I am being *called* to do.

Being a woman has especially helped me to understand that true leadership does not need a formal title. In the church, where women are excluded from some of the most prominent leadership roles, I can still live out the threefold nature of my baptism in profound ways. As a part of my *priestly* vocation, I am called to "make holy" the places and spaces in which I find myself. This includes my family, my social circles, my workplace, my community, and the larger society. I can do this by committing to carrying the light of Christ into every situation. In my *prophetic* vocation I am called to speak on God's behalf. I must watch and listen for God in our world and point it out to others. I am invited to teach others about how God is moving and doing something new. I can do this by accompanying others on their faith journeys and helping them discern God's presence in their own lives. I do not even need to be employed by the church to do this. In fact, I observe as hundreds of volunteers and ministry leaders in my parish community do this week after week! As a part of my *kingly* call, governing from a place of servant leadership means ensuring that all people have what they need to grow into the person God created them to be. I can be an advocate for justice, I can help make connections and use my network to serve others, and I can contribute in a personal way by accompanying people with the support and care they need.

In addition, as a wife and mother I also exercise a unique role of leadership within my family. My four children, especially my two daughters, are watching me grow into the woman God has called me to be. I am leading by my example every day. I am showing them how a baptized Christian lives. I am teaching them to recognize who they are and whose they are, all the while showing them that every single person is created in the image and likeness of God and bears a piece of the divine that the world needs. They are listening to me as I talk to them about injustice, poverty, discrimination, homophobia, xenophobia, and so on. They accompany me as I engage in works of mercy and now, as we are in the tenuous "teen years," I pray some of this stays with them.

What challenges do women face as leaders in Catholic ministries? How have you engaged these challenges?

The challenges women face as leaders in Catholic ministries are many, and engaging these topics in constructive ways is difficult. For me, one of the most frustrating challenges has been watching as women are not invited to the table or are not given a chance to express their views. At times, I have been the only woman present when matters of import to the parish community were being discussed. In addition to the male clerics at the table, often the directors of high-profile roles—liturgy and music, operations, finance, community outreach, and school principal—were all men. Representation matters. While the majority of the "worker bees" at parishes in which I have ministered (coordinators and administrative specialists) are women, the major leadership positions have been mostly held by men. The staffing decisions of the parish should reflect the fact that typically at least 50 percent of the community is female. I have engaged this issue by making a point to inquire if other women can be invited into important conversations. When we have staffing discussions, I advocate for the consideration of adding women to our roster. It feels awkward sometimes to be "that person," bringing up uncomfortable issues, but if I do not speak up, who will?

In my response to the prior question I spoke about just wages. At one parish in which I worked, I discovered that I was being paid between 30 percent and 50 percent less than some of my male peers, many of whom had less experience and education than I. I raised this issue with the pastor and human resources coordinator as a justice issue, but it was brushed off. Excuses of offertory being down, personal stewardship, and "time to figure it out" were given, but there was no affirmation of the injustice and certainly no apology. After speaking to other female colleagues, I know that I am not the only one who has had this experience. I believe this often happens because many of those who are in ministry are women and they often have a spouse who is the primary breadwinner for the home (or at least makes enough money to allow the woman to accept a less just salary). This must change. If the church values the contributions of female employees, it must compensate them justly.

Condescension and misogyny are another two issues with which I have struggled, and after speaking with some other female friends and colleagues I know that this is not an issue for the church setting alone. While my male lay ministry peers have generally treated me with respect throughout my career, much of my experience in dealing with the "non-ministry" employees (for example, finance, operations, communications) has been navigating persistent condescension. Many of these men I have encountered came to work in parishes post-retirement, following a career in the business world or in another industry. While I believe that they are mostly unaware of how their actions affect others, their behavior still has a clear impact, especially on the morale of women in the organization. I have had many interactions with these men, across multiple parishes, where my opinions and even knowledge have been discounted and I have been treated or spoken to in a patronizing manner. I am stubborn, however, and have worked even more diligently to arm myself with facts and educate myself about whatever topic is being discussed. I have learned to speak up, to ask questions, and to constructively disagree. This is perhaps one of the most challenging pieces of being in parish leadership, but my endeavors are worthwhile because I can see how I have contributed to slowly changing culture and clearing a path for others.

Another challenge that women in leadership contend with is difficulty building relationships with male collaborators. Over the years I have found that it is hard to forge bonds with some clerics with whom I work, because I am a woman and the social opportunities for interaction are limited. Often I have heard male staff members speak of how Father took them out for a beer or for lunch. It is over these drinks and meals that lives are shared and relationships are forged. As a woman, I find I have been excluded from these types of outings because it simply would not be "proper" for me to be out, one on one, with a priest. I know that there is little I can do to change this thinking, but I have addressed it with male colleagues over the years and have challenged them to find ways to include women. Because we are not invited to participate in these outings with clerics, we need help in finding other ways to build relationships. Forging these relationships of trust and mutual understanding is important. When they are missing, I have found myself being kept at arm's length and treated with a lack of warmth and genuineness during interactions. There was one cleric I encountered who was terrified of women, suggesting that female staff members might try to seduce him if he were ever alone with us. Sadly, our church's unhealthy relationship with sexuality does not help this situation.

The most disappointing challenge I have faced as a woman in ministry leadership is a lack of understanding from several pastors. Because the leaders of parishes are priests, and male by default, there is someone at the top of every community who simply does not grasp the unique struggles and lived experience of about 50 percent of our congregants. These pastors have lived and moved in a male-dominated environment for their entire adult lives, and it is my experience that they possess little frame of reference for what it means to be "woman." Unfortunately, I have found that many priests with whom I have worked have not even considered their limited viewpoint. Whenever I have had the opportunity, I have attempted to engage pastors in conversation around the unique struggles I have experienced as a woman in ministry: harassment, suspicion, dismissal, discrimination, unfair pay, and so on. I am hoping that repeatedly bringing these topics to light will eventually lead to understanding.

In your view, what skills, behavior, and temperament are important to leadership? How would you describe yourself on these dimensions?

For me, leadership is about service—putting oneself both in the service of people in an organization and in the service of the organization itself. Especially in the church, leaders should always be pointing others to Christ and should always be cultivating their own relationships with Jesus. Leaders should be inclusive, noticing who is not at the table and creating room for them. In addition, leaders should identify and develop giftedness in followers. Skills that are important for leaders to develop include emotional intelligence, communication and interpersonal skills, relational and pastoral skills, time management and organizational skills, flexibility and versatility, visioning, prayer leadership, and discernment of the Spirit.

Leaders must lead by example, as change usually comes from the top of an organization. This means adopting a spirit of humility and searching, taking on a learning posture and an openness to the ideas of others. They should operate in a mode of collaboration and gentleness instead of domination and aggressiveness. Leaders should model a life of prayer and a relationship with Christ, especially in the sacraments. They should be a mirror, reflecting the light of Jesus no matter the situation. Leaders also need to be sure they are physically, emotionally, and spiritually taking care of themselves. As the saying goes, you can't pour from an empty cup. Sleep, good nutrition, exercise, quiet time, days off, retreats, mental-health counseling, and spiritual direction are all things a leader should be considering if not taking advantage of.

Through self-study, I have discovered what my own dominant leadership traits and behaviors are. While these traits are positive and help to serve the organization, they can also have a shadow side and be a potential cause of derailment. Being attentive to the self-care practices above helps avoid going off the rails. First, I am an organizer and driven to plan in an orderly and strategic manner. This has been useful in helping a team to work toward a vision and making expectations clear. People with whom I work respond well to a deliberate roadmap, goals broken down into smaller steps, and knowing where we are headed. In addition, this trait serves well in meetings as plans ensure good steward-ship of everyone's time. When this trait goes awry, however, my drive has the potential to set expectations that are unrealistic and unachievable, causing others to become sidelined and ultimately give up or become indifferent.

One of my leadership mantras is "relationship first," and I pride myself on honesty, authenticity, and sincerity in relation-ships, offering individualized attention to followers as needed as a coach, mentor, and cheerleader. Employees and volunteers have shared how much this has meant to them, that I care for them as people and not just as a means to an end. This also helps to build incredible amounts of trust not only within my own team but across others. At times, however, my desire to be in relationship with followers has the potential to become unbalanced as I give more and more of myself over to coaching and mentoring. This can lead to my own emotional burnout as well as the creation of unhealthy boundaries with followers. The good news of this "relationship first" approach to employees and volunteers is that I place a high value on interactions with people and in building healthy relationships with them that ultimately serve their own well being and success. This, in turn, is crucial to the achievement of organizational goals. Affirmed, connected, appreciated, coached followers ultimately lead to successful leaders and organizations. The greatest assets of organizations are its members. I have a deep appreciation of giftedness in others and take seriously St. Paul's metaphor that we are all parts of the body of Christ. Each person has something unique to contribute to the success of an organization, and others' gifts do not take away from my own. Bringing together a group of people and watching them use their respective gifts to vision or solve a problem is one of my favorite things to do. A difficulty in this can be finding the right people with the right gifts for the right situations. While this is no easy task, by leading with a balance of pastoral skills and healthy relationships, the teams I lead have been able to accomplish incredible ministry.

What is the role of power in leadership? In your experience, what are the sources of power? Do men and women come into power and exercise power differently?

If power is the ability that one person has to influence another, then a leader's power is an important asset. Leaders can leverage their power to motivate, to better the individual or group, or to accomplish something in the group. I believe that when leaders' power is derived from relationship to and care for their followers, how their followers view them as an expert, and how they support followers in accomplishing their goals and tasks, it is the most ethical and effective use of power. The power comes from a place of attraction and expertise. There is a shadow side to power, however. When those who are in power exploit and coerce those who are dependent upon them, it is a negative, unethical use of power.

Power comes from different places. It can come from controlling "rewards" like bonuses, time off, promotions, and so forth, or coercion in that the person in power is able to make things unpleasant for another. It can also originate from a place of legitimacy in that the person with power has the "right" to influence because of position or title. In addition, expertise can give power as well as a person's desire to be like the person in power or their identification with the person in power.[1]

The power that I have found most helpful in ministry is legitimate power, the mode of power that Jesus most often leveraged. Jesus attracted followers who wanted to be like him and identified with him. This gave him influence over his followers. Those of us in ministry should gravitate toward this type of power, as we should lead by our example. We may also exercise power from our place of expertise, but we must keep in mind that being a follower of Jesus is not about knowledge. We must be careful not to blur those lines for our followers.

In the church I have seen the use of power played out in negative ways. While there are usually no rewards or bonuses to be given out to employees in a parish, those in leadership roles can leverage coercive power by making life miserable for those around them. Legitimate power also plays a role in the church in that the ordained have the "right" to influence others. This is not only an issue for the ordained, however. I have encountered lay people who also exercise their right to be in power in a negative way. When titles and positions are given, ego and agenda can often get in the way.

In my experience, men and women in the church do come into power differently. As women cannot be ordained, they are excluded from the ability to influence that comes with the position of an ordained minister. I cannot count how many times I have taught on a subject or answered a question and had a parishioner say, "Let's see what Father has to say about that." I could present on the most interesting, most engaging opportunity for

---

[1] See J. R. P. French Jr. and B. Raven, "The Bases of Social Power," in *Studies in Social Power*, ed. D. Cartwright, 150–67 (Ann Arbor: University of Michigan Press, 1959).

formation, and the priests would get more of an audience talking about the process of choosing the paint color for the sanctuary! But women do tend to be excellent relationship builders, and that is where a lot of their power comes from in ministry.

When it comes to wielding influence, I have noticed that several male counterparts do so by either appearing more knowledgeable in a subject area or appearing physically more powerful by the voice, delivery, and posture they use. They tend to be more combative and more likely to challenge in meetings. In contrast, I have observed that many of my female counterparts wield influence by building collaborative relationships and attempting to reach consensus. Their power often comes from information that they gather by listening and observing.

Were there mentors who contributed to your success? If so, in what ways? Have you mentored other women? If so, in what ways? What advice would you offer to women looking to work in and eventually lead a Catholic ministry?

The list of female mentors who have contributed to my success is long, but a few stand out in my mind. Catzel LaVecchia was my high school youth minister and identified my own giftedness when I could not see any worth in myself. She helped me to cultivate my gifts and recognize my vocation to ministry. She talked me through the early years of my career and became so much more than a mentor. Now she is a colleague, a companion on the journey, a cheerleader, and a sister.

I was privileged to work alongside Katherine Angulo when she was diocesan director of youth ministry in the Diocese of Raleigh for a number of years. Katherine taught me about persistence, how to dream big and have the courage to ask God for miraculous things in faith, how to navigate a leadership role in a male-dominated organization, and how to deal creatively with conflict. Katherine is an example of a woman who gives others a "hand up." She continues to be a dear friend and collaborator. She is truly a gift to the church.

In grad school I was fortunate to sit at the feet of some amazing women: Dr. Marti Jewell, who taught me so much about relational ministry and doing "deeper listening" to the Spirit; Dr. Diana Dudoit Raiche, whose academic command of catechesis is incomparable and who helped me dream about my future; and Dr. Jodi Hunt, who mentored me through a huge catechetical project. These brilliant women were kind but demanding professors, forming me in how to be prophetic, how to challenge the status quo from within the structure, and how to make my voice heard. They are each a unique Spirit-driven model of female leadership, and I am so much better for having been mentored by them.

I am fairly certain that my maternal grandmother, Anne, prayed me into my vocation with the thousands of Rosaries she would say for me over the years. She is the one who inspired my love for the Blessed Mother and taught me that one can lead from any situation, especially by example. She loved unconditionally and understood the value of human suffering because she carried so much of it herself. I have her to thank for much of my emotional intelligence. At an early age she instilled in me that my feelings were my own and there was no right way to feel but that actions were what really mattered.

My mother, Joanne, would balk at anyone calling her a leader or mentor, but she has been an example of "doing what you can with what you have" and, like my grandmother, leading from wherever you are. For years, Mom put her own education and career on the back burner so she could care for her children. When we were old enough, she juggled work and college courses, and eventually became a CPA, traveling the globe as an international auditor. Her example to me of balancing family needs with her own needs is still a yardstick for my own life. She is also never afraid to admit her shortcomings and continues to learn and better herself even in her retirement years. She just informed me she signed up for banjo lessons!

Having been formed by so many women over the years, it is always a privilege to pay it forward and give a "hand up." As a youth minister I was privileged to walk with hundreds of teens and adult volunteers, teaching them about God's love, forming them in peer leadership, working with them on telling their own faith stories, and leading by example. I have also mentored a number of young men and women whom I have hired to work on my teams over the years. Part of my role as a leader is to ensure that there is a succession plan for the organization, and I am keenly aware of the need to form the next generation for ministry. The mentoring includes not only what programs look like and how to do ministry but also how to be in relationship with God and with others. For the women who work for me, I see one of my main roles as protecting their vocations. While many are called to married and family life, they are also called to ministry. I try to create a workplace environment where they do not have to choose between the two, figuring out creative and flexible ways for them to faithfully answer God's call in their lives.

What advice do I give these up-and-coming leaders? I was chatting over these questions with one of my colleagues, and I jokingly said the advice I would give to a woman looking to get into ministry was, "Run." We had a good laugh but agreed that this vocation is not for the faint of heart. I believe a woman must have a strong sense of self to be able to work in an organization where women are not admitted to the highest levels of leadership. Perseverance is important because many situations can be frustrating and often out of our control. One thing I always tell myself is to keep my "eyes on the prize." Ministry is a vocation, and if one has that call then there is something that God has for us to do. When days are particularly rough, I try to recount the times that I saw Christ, and it is almost always in the people I

work with or serve. This helps me refocus on what really matters. Building relationships with others in the field also helps
on tough days, not only to share ideas but to help carry one
another's burdens and share joys. Talk to women who have been
in ministry for a long time; sit at their feet and learn from them.

Also, I tell them to never stop learning. Read books and articles and see what others are doing. Go to conferences. Watch
webinars. Much of ministry is borrowing the ideas and best
practices of others and making them your own. Pray. Spend time
with the word. One of the easiest ways to start out is to spend
a little time with the daily Lectionary readings. The Liturgy of
the Hours is fantastic for this as well. Start with one of the times
of the day. (I like Evening Prayer best.) Give yourself at least ten
minutes of unplugged silence every day (get in your car in the
driveway if you have to or lock yourself in the bathroom and
turn on the shower for white noise). Develop a rich sacramental
life. Go to daily mass, eucharistic adoration, and reconciliation
when you can. All that grace is yours to receive.

It is also helpful to do some self-reflection and take personal
assessments. Find out what *really* makes you tick, how you lead,
how you communicate, how you receive information, how you
interact with others, and then make an action plan and put
practices in place to set yourself up for success in these areas.
Ultimately, though, go easy on yourself! Remember that you
are a precious child of God, created in God's own image with
immeasurable value and dignity. When you do not get it right
or fall down, give yourself a moment to recover, and then get
up. Do not stay down. You have a piece of the divine within you
that the world needs—listen to the voice of the Spirit calling
you forward.

28

Leadership for Healing

Sister Donna Markham, OP

As I think about my experience as a woman who has had the opportunity to serve in a number of leadership positions, both within and outside the Catholic Church, what strikes me is that I have never actually conceptualized my "style" of leadership as being unique to me as a woman. Rather, I am a leader whose gender happens to be female. What I share here are my thoughts as a woman of faith about what it means for me to strive to be as effective as I can be as an organizational leader.

A while back the journal *American Psychologist* devoted an entire issue to the topic of leadership. Perhaps one of the more provocative articles concerned developments in a systems model of leadership based on the research of R. J. Sternberg. Sternberg identified three key components of leadership: *wisdom, intelligence,* and *creativity.* The research indicated that these three components working together in a wonderful synthesis compose the foundation for the highly effective leader.

I might rephrase this from my own perspective by saying that leadership infused with holy Wisdom, God's feminine spirit, is directed toward enfleshing the practice of the reign of God in our world. God's reign draws all creation into communion; it pulls us human beings into action on behalf of the good that we hold in common; it invites us into community, into reverent communion. But the practice of the reign of God seems so far from our reality today. If there were ever a time when wise leaders are needed to counter our pull toward further shattering relationships and fracturing community, it is now. We have come face to face with our sin—the consequences of broken connections that have splintered global and national civil discourse. We live in the midst of extravagant ruptures in which we unwittingly collude, and it is very uncomfortable and terribly frightening. But it is into this reality that we are called to lead and to minister—a moment in history where we seem balanced on a precipice between the ending of all that the modern era told us we could count on and the dawn of a tumultuous, mysterious postmodern world where so many things are questioned or actually in the process of being debunked and deconstructed.

Leadership today is neither about trying frantically to rescue the tenets of modernity nor about a naive, uncritical accommodation to the postmodern discourse. I believe it is about the evangelization, the making holy, of our culture as it unfolds in this time. God's holy Wisdom guides that process in my life. It is the aspiration to that guidance that drives any role of leadership I have been privileged to exercise.

Spiritual depth, emotional maturity, and intellectual capacity are requisites to *engaging* postmodern deconstruction with gospel-focused reconstruction. The "answer" to the postmodern reality is not to try to destroy it in some futile effort to recapture bygone days, but rather to engage it, to work within it, to strengthen what is healing and noble in this unfolding global reality so that it might be directed toward the good that we hold in common. In other words, the effective leader must have the ability to *engage the gospel in dialogue with the culture*. I believe this is at the core of the "new evangelization, building the civilization of love"—as then Cardinal Ratzinger titled his paper on the subject.[1] This is highly relational work.

Leading on behalf of the common good is as radical as it is countercultural in this climate. It takes courage to step into a pervasive momentum that is pulling us apart and dare to do something otherwise. Leaders who are filled with God's holy Wisdom inspire others to take a risk on behalf of the common good, on behalf of the mission of Jesus, and are willing to do so themselves—put their life on the line for the sake of protecting and fostering the connections, establishing relationships among all those whom we serve.

I recall listening to an NPR account of Wesley Autrey, a fifty-year-old construction worker who jumped onto the New York subway tracks in the face of the headlights of an oncoming train to save a stranger who had stumbled off the platform. Crazy—or profoundly holy? How do we make the decision to do the right thing, the ethical thing, the holy thing? Mr. Autrey somehow knew. He acted instinctively. He connected with another human being, someone who was unfamiliar and unknown. And he saved a life. Wise leadership in these times is about sensing the urgency of the moment and taking action that will serve the greater good, regardless of the consequences. Faced with the enormity of the humanitarian disaster resulting from the pandemic, it is a right and moral decision to reflect on the extent of our great-heartedness, our generosity to our sisters and brothers in need, our love and respect for those who are suffering.

In this way I would venture to say that leaders have a particular obligation to be catalysts for a "new evangelization" grounded in love and reconciliation rather than becoming mired

---

[1] See Cardinal Ratzinger, "The New Evangelization, Building the Civilization of Love," Address to Catechists and Religion Teachers, December 12, 2000.

in proving themselves "right" or "playing it safe." This includes witnessing to and calling others to uncompromising participation in the mission of Jesus, holding our communities to truthfulness and integrity, promoting dialogue across all kinds of difficult and contentious topics, and leading in forgiveness. Given the enormity of this task in light of today's reality, I believe one of the most crucial skills wise leaders must learn and undertake is to promote the healing of the ruptures that surround us on all sides. This reconciling behavior necessitates our taking an entirely different approach toward dealing with conflicts, differences, and dissension. Everything we should be engaged in doing as leaders today must be focused on connecting across divisions and discord and working through fractured relationships and broken connections among us.

We know all too well that the lack of connection is the breeding ground for violence. This has happened in our country far too often. We can each recall examples. It has sometimes happened even in our church, when judgments and litmus tests are used against one other to determine who is faithful or orthodox or authentic or who is considered closed-minded or reactionary or liberal. We have engaged in some dangerous name-calling behaviors that have broken us apart and threaten to fragment us further. There are people we are afraid to talk with because we are afraid we will be hurt. There are likely people who are afraid to talk with us for the very same reason. There is a deep sadness resident in these situations.

Wesley Autrey didn't evaluate how different from himself the man was who fell onto the subway tracks. He didn't hesitate because the man was of a different race and age cohort. He didn't wait until he could talk him out of the predicament he was in. He didn't take the time to assess the risks to his own well being. He acted in the urgency of the moment, and he acted to protect the value of a person's life.

In some metaphorical way we are globally facing the terror of an oncoming train that is being powered by the energy of hatred and self-serving judgmentalism and fear—and we intuitively realize the only way we are going to avert further disaster is if we take action on behalf of one another. This is terribly countercultural. It is the radical message of the gospel facing us head on. And it's our choice to determine if we will listen this time. Another way of saying this is that universal communion, living in deliberate relatedness, must outweigh any intent we have of overpowering the different "other" in order to protect our own comforts. In essence, leadership must be directed toward community building through conflicts of all kinds—whether in our families, in our workplaces, in our parishes, or in our international discourse.

Effective leaders must be willing to engage differences; to engage in conversation with those who disagree or dislike or frighten us; to work with conflict in such a way that ruptures are mended and community is promoted. Determining what can be done to sustain the relationship with the disagreeing or different other is far more important than determining strategies for winning some argument or proving that we are right. The gospel is filled with accounts of Jesus engaging in dialogue and establishing relationships with characters with whom he likely has serious problems—adulteresses, tax collectors, sinners, and nonbelievers. He does not try to convince these people to think and believe what he does. He simply loves them. Love establishes relationship with the differing, even faltering, other. Love always outweighs righteousness for him.

The significance of connecting through dialogue has become a field of study for many people concerned about the precarious nature of our world. Scientist David Bohm pushes us to discover our connections through multifaceted dialogues that illuminate the underlying unity among us. One of the greatest physicists and thinkers of the twentieth century, he wrote in *On Dialogue,* "Love will go away if we can't communicate and share meaning. . . . If we can really communicate, then we will have fellowship, participation, friendship and love. . . . Such an energy has been called 'communion.'"[2] While David Bohm could not have imagined the danger of these times, he knew at some profound level how essential it is for us to foster community through our conflicts and differences. *Love will go away if we can't communicate.*

Establishing a relationship of mutual respect frees us to manage our differences. It requires that we acknowledge we do not possess the whole truth of a situation and that we have something to learn from someone else. It calls for a certain humility. In listening with openness to the opposing other, I begin to learn how perspectives have been formulated and what experiences lay beneath a given position. At the same time I open myself to the vulnerable act of sharing some of my own history, study, and prayer as these have fashioned my varying perspective. Respectful communication strengthens connections as the fragile bonds of community begin to form. In this way we begin to assuage vestiges of hostility.

Our work as leaders today is about striving to connect people in a positive way, people who have widely differing views about important matters but who are all invested in promoting the common goods of life, respect, mercy, and forgiveness. Parties who are willing to enter into this alternative mode of managing differences step outside cold standoffs and determined avoidance of one another. They move beyond violence in efforts to search for what unifies rather than divides. This is about witnessing to the reign of God—and it is truly a very courageous act. This is what it means to lead.

---

[2] David Bohm, *On Dialogue,* Routledge Classics, vol. 76 (New York: Routledge, 1996), 46–47.

Leading in compassion, with a fierce sense of mission, implies moving away from the separate "I's" toward the promise of a connected "we." In our accustomed autonomous, and often righteous, individualistic life stance, this becomes very challenging. It is posited on the promise of community. Members of the community of believers who have placed our lives in deliberate service to the mission of the gospel cannot, in all integrity, do otherwise. When we dare to take the steps toward becoming a "we" despite our differences, we are making a commitment to route out any cynicism that serves to block trust. That means we cast aside thinking there are ulterior motives to engaging in the dialogue or some hidden agendas that are cleverly sequestered just under the common ground we seek to stand upon.

Unfortunately, just as not everyone is willing to be engaged wholeheartedly in the mission of the gospel, not everyone is able to be an effective leader in contentious times. Perhaps the first and foremost requisite is the openness to move toward deeper personal and communal freedom. In other words, I believe this is a commitment to accept an invitation to ongoing conversion—and we all know that conversion is painful because it entails significant letting go of what has become quite comfortable and accommodating. Such an attitude of the heart and soul is foundational to being a leader in faith today. Besides a grounding in spirituality, faith leaders need to possess maturity and fundamental psychological health, a grounded sense of humility that ensures respect for others as peers, and a commitment to rigorous study and reflection.

When leaders are unafraid to engage a contentious culture from this vantage point, they become agents of healing who invite their communities to a more palpable participation in the mission of Jesus. They serve as signs of hope in a world that cries out for reconciliation and peace. Leadership today must be about connecting. It necessarily is about engaging others in the sacred work of creating universal communion that begins to assuage the ruptures so prevalent around us. In the midst of conflict we can never stop the dialogue as we strive to make adversaries partners. Leading is about recognizing and reminding the community that we are all connected, that we reside alongside one another, and that to harm another is ultimately self-damaging. Leadership, when all is said and done, is realizing this connection through all our differences, a connection that leads us to awe and makes reverence our only rational response to one another.

In summary, I would say that a reliance on holy Wisdom, on community building, on the commitment to repair ruptures, on a certain fearlessness, and on a passion for the mission of the gospel are fundamental to what I believe as a leader. Is that unique to me because I am a woman? I doubt it. Has the fact that I am a woman had an influence on how I have come to espouse these values? Perhaps. Because I am a woman, am I more attuned to relational dimensions of leadership? I'm not convinced, but maybe. And, yes, I have been challenged by some male counterparts who perceive my leadership style to be "feminist" or "too soft." Others have told me I am "too strong." My learning with those mixed reviews simply confirms my resolve to rely on prayer, to be who I am called to be, and to do the best I can to promote God's reign.

Closing Words

Carolyn Y. Woo

When I started this book I was aware of quite a number of women leaders with whom I had worked or networked. However, I was still surprised by the high percentages of women who serve as leaders of different Catholic ministries, as reported in Chapter 1. That women are restricted from ordained ministries does not necessarily mean that their talents are disregarded or that their contributions have no impact.

The church lives not only through worship and sacrament, but in the many ministries of care, education, and healing. These render Jesus's love real and present, and animate the words of the gospel. In addition, women's work of evangelization in and out of the family has built the foundation on which youngsters and neighbors come to understand, internalize, and practice their faith. To downplay women's work and ministries is clericalism, whether the attitude is held by lay people or clergy, men or women.

While the leadership of women in Catholic ministries is noteworthy, the consideration and appointment of women as leaders is not yet routine across the church. Women's leadership is not yet 50 percent in most ministries, and not at proportions equal to the number of women who populate many pastoral, social service, and educational institutions.

We need more women to step up. But they are unlikely to do so if they are not aware of the opportunities and do not sense that they are wanted and valued. The first condition is easy to remedy: the lack of information about leadership opportunities. That is the motivation for this book. On the other hand, knowing is not the same as doing. As I mentioned in the Introduction, I hope this book makes it difficult for women of faith to walk away from service to or a career in church ministries. Our disappointments can be reasons to step out or reasons to step in.

The second condition would require a change in communication and behavior by which clergy and church leaders express their respect and appreciation, not only for women, but for lay people in general. How they get to know, genuinely listen to, invite, actively engage, and account to the community sets the tone for whether lay people are family or guests. The adage "pray, pay, and obey" would be humorous if it did not so pervasively dominate the perception and response of parishioners and, I suspect, shape the expectations of some clergy. The messenger is the message and the requisite source of change.

In the end, the extension of opportunities for women to serve as leaders is not first and foremost for the enhancement of workforce diversity or access to a talent pool. Nor is it only about the work of the church. It is about the very identity of the church itself. Church, as the body of Christ, requires us to be one: men, women, lay, ordained. It is not by our own accord that we reach across, look for the good in the other, and recognize our own limited understanding. Grace takes the next step, but grace is there for the asking.

As Walter Brueggemann has said: "What God does first, best, and most is to trust people with their moment in history. God trusts us to do what must be done for the sake of the whole community."[1]

---

[1] Walter Brueggemann, "The Trusted Creature," *Catholic Biblical Quarterly* 31 (1969): 488.

Acknowledgments

This book came about from the encouragement and guidance of many wise and generous advisers. I start with my editor, Robert Ellsberg, whose immediate and enthusiastic acceptance of the book concept set me confidently and resolutely on my course. Consultations with good friends, sung and unsung laborers in the ministries of the Catholic Church, helped me sketch the map for this book. Thank you to Fr. Bryan Hehir, Professor Catherine Hilkert, Professor John Cavadini and his team at the McGrath Institute, Barbara McCrabb, Mary Pat Donoghue, Professor Zeni Fox, Greg Erlandson, John Carr, Sr. Mary Haddad, Fr. Dennis Holtschneider, Professor Ann Astell, and Professor Kathleen Sprow Cummings. A special dinner is owed Jan Jenkins, my neighbor, who supported me with the loan of books, labor of editing, and spirited advocacy for women in the church.

Sixteen women leaders who were willing to share their personal journeys in autobiographical essays greatly enriched this book. They also served as my thinking partners by their responses to the themes I posted. Their voices and experiences provided a mosaic that I alone could not have.

This book is informed by personal experiences of faith and work, both in and outside the church. My thoughts stem from a personal gestalt encompassing the formation of faith and how I have come to understand church. Foundational to my faith are the Maryknoll Sisters, to whom I dedicate this book. I learned less from the catechism or our classes in biblical knowledge and more from watching how people live their faith—what they do in relation to what the Bible says, how they treat one another, how they find fulfillment.

The answers I got that turned me to God come from gentle spiritual giants among my teachers: Sister Helene O'Sullivan, Sr. Marylou Teufel, Sr. Virginia Flagg, and Sr. Ann Carol Brielmaier.

St. Thomas Aquinas Center at Purdue University claimed me as sister and daughter when I had no kin on campus. Its commitment to fostering an adult faith in step with the intellectual life at a university nurtured both my husband and me and established the values and priorities of our marriage. My sense of Church, despite all the breaches, scandals, and disappointments, is forever anchored in the grace of God, of which I have been a recipient through the ministries of Fr. Leo Piguet, Fr. Leo Haigherty, Mary Pat Siczek Young, Fr. Phil Bowers, and Fr. Dave Hellman.

I have learned that the first gesture of church, the body of Christ, must be welcome. At the University of Notre Dame, hospitality is the charism of its founding order, the Congregation of Holy Cross (CSC). From the beginning our family was adopted by the universal pastor of South Bend, Fr. Paul Doyle, CSC, and my work at the business school was accelerated by Fr. Bill Beauchamp, CSC, before I could establish a track record. Spiritual guidance from Fr. Ted Hesburgh, CSC, to always invoke the Holy Spirit and from Fr. Ken Molinaro, CSC, to fashion my compass by joys and fears became the touchstones for my ministries. The CSC community nurtured the faith of our two sons.

In my spiritual growth I am deeply inspired by the lives and works of fellow Christians. Their service to the poor, advocacy for the marginalized, marches for the oppressed, and affirmation of one another are manifestations of communion, of what it means to be one in Christ. They are my companions, jointly discerning and responding to the call of God.

This book reminds us that, despite our frustration and the desire to see more and faster, women's leadership in Catholic ministries would not be possible without the support and personal sponsorship of some among the clergy and the episcopacy. Opportunities have to be provided and confidence expressed. In my own experience I am grateful to Fr. Monk Malloy, CSC, and Fr. John Jenkins, CSC, who respectively offered me leadership platforms as dean of the Mendoza College of Business and coordinator of the Vatican Dialogues on Energy Transition.

Catholic Relief Services was governed by a board of all clergy until Bishop Bob Lynch proposed and the US Conference of Catholic Bishops approved the composition of twelve lay and thirteen bishop board members. This change significantly broke open the involvement of women and eventually my appointment as CEO of CRS. CRS operated in complicated settings requiring board resolution of tough issues straddling different cultural ideologies. With candor, respect, and careful steps, the board was able to address these issues without rupture and neglect of the mission to serve the most vulnerable.

A leader cannot succeed or enjoy work amid opposing demands without genuine support and open communication with the board chair. For that, I am most grateful for the CRS board chairs who guided and supported me in my tenure: Bishop Jerry Kicanas, Archbishop Paul Coakley, and Bishop Gregory Mansour. Their guidance demonstrates how the church can come together with grace in the Holy Spirit. During my lowest moments, when false accusations were made against CRS, Bishop Kicanas stood with us to understand the issues, get to the truth, and engage the Bishops' Conference to issue a statement of support. Having witnessed a moment of unity among the bishops, I know the division we currently experience is not the only way.

The leadership journey is more likely to happen with the help of mentors. They spot talent, invest themselves in the development of these colleagues, offer opportunities, and provide counsel when needed. I have been blessed by extraordinary mentors every step of the way. My first counselor at Purdue, Professor Glenn Griffin, allowed me to sign up for as many credit hours and across as many departments as I requested. My major professor, Arnie Cooper, took me by the hand on the fine crafts of case teaching and research publishing, and nominated me for positions that launched me in the field. The provost at Purdue, Dr. Robert Ringel, enlisted me as associate provost, assigned me to lead university-level projects, and took me to Big Ten provost meetings. Whenever I pleaded lack of experience, he would remind me that people do not look at me for what I cannot do, but for what I can do. Dr. Steven Beering, president of Purdue University, continued to nominate me for key positions even after I left the university. His advocacy led to my first public-company board directorship. Nathan Hatch, president emeritus of Wake Forest University, recruited me to Notre Dame when he was provost. Nathan became my gold standard for how to listen for obstacles that prevent progress and how to use the president's perch for removing obstacles. He was a true believer in talent and was therefore creative in how to recruit and support it.

Mentors are not only those who hold higher positions. Equally important are colleagues who contribute to our success, often with little benefit to themselves except the intrinsic satisfaction of seeing others and the organization flourish. Whatever advice they gave, I took it as gold. To Logan Jordan, Bill Nichols, Leo Burke, Ed Trubac, Roger Huang, Sean Callahan, Annemarie Reilly, Mark Melia, Mark Palmer, Jean Simmons, Pat Medich, Winnie Walters, Nancy Cole, and Carol Bobick: thank you.

This book identifies the capacity for the other as a critical requirement for leadership. I first learned this from my family. As Pope Francis often teaches, family is our first teacher. There is a Chinese adage about family that goes like this: "If one has rice, we all have rice; if there is only rice soup, we will have rice soup together." As my father often reminded us: we Chinese do